LAW, LABOUR AND SOCIETY IN

From repression to reluct

Anthony Woodiwiss

London and New York

First published 1992
by Routledge
11 New Fetter Lane, London EC4P 4EE

Simultaneously published in the USA and Canada
by Routledge
a division of Routledge, Chapman and Hall, Inc.
29 West 35th Street, New York, NY 10001

Typeset in Palatino by Michael Mepham, Frome, Somerset
Printed and bound in Great Britain by
Biddles Ltd, Guildford and King's Lynn

British Library Cataloguing in Publication Data
Woodiwiss, Anthony
  Law, Labour and Society in Japan: From Repression
  to Reluctant Recognition
  I. Title
  952.048
  ISBN 0–415–06842–8

Library of Congress Cataloging in Publication Data
Woodiwiss, Anthony
  Law, Labour and Society in Japan: From Repression
  to Reluctant Recognition/ Anthony Woodiwiss
  Includes bibliographical references and index
  ISBN 0–415–06842–8
  1. Labor laws and legislation–Japan–History 2. Industrial
  relations–Japan–History I. Title
  344.52'01—dc20
  [345.2041]

To Rachel and Helen
And to Lennox, Kathleen, Joanne, Kurt,
Valerie, Sandra and Mwasi

CONTENTS

ACKNOWLEDGEMENTS

As I sit down to perform the final and most pleasurable of an author's tasks, it is immediately clear to me that it is going to take longer than usual. This is because I am suddenly aware that I have required far more help in more areas than has been the case with my previous books. It is a tribute to all those I am about to name that this realisation occurs only now.

My first debt is to Sybile Van Der Sprenkel, who first stimulated my interest in Japan by her lectures at the University of Leeds some twenty-five years ago. I had no idea then how regrettably rare it was for non-specialist students to have the opportunity to study Japan in a British university – recently things have changed for the better, but not much.

The greatest single debt incurred in the writing of this book is that which I owe to William Gould IV of Stanford University. In a gesture of quite exceptional academic generosity, Professor Gould allowed a total stranger to photocopy the collection of case report translations that he had assembled, with what must have been considerable difficulty, in connection with the writing of his own pathbreaking study of Japanese labour law. It is appropriate, therefore, that I repeat his thanks to the following for their translations: Beth Cary, Michael Lewis, Andrew Goble, Hitomi Tonomura, David Groth, Kent Gilbert, Donna Jean Albright, Roderick Seeman, Thomas Nevins and, finally, Conan Grames and his team at Baker McKenzie (Tokyo).

I am also greatly indebted in a more diffuse way to my friends amongst the Japanese sociological community who, both as visiting scholars at the University of Essex and/or in Japan, shared their several and diverse knowledges of their society with me. Particular thanks are due to the following: Arisue Ken of Keio University, Fujimori Shonosuke of Okayama University, Fuwa Kazuhiko of Tohoku University, Harada Katsu of Meiji Gakuin University, Shimodaira Hiromi of Shinshu University and Watanabe Masao of Hitotsobashi University.

Thanks are also due to my friends and colleagues in the two universities between which I have divided my time over the past five years. At Dokkyo I am particularly grateful to Professors Akiyama, Ishiyama, Kuwahara, Matsushima, Hayashi, Hagiwara and, a fellow Visiting Professor, Franz Neusheler of Duisberg University and the Willy Brandt Foundation. I am also most grateful for the friendship and consideration shown me by many members of the administrative staff at Dokkyo, especially Minami Yuzo, Nishida Gen and Yoshida Chiharu. At Essex all of my colleagues have been their highly supportive selves. With regard to the present project, special thanks are due to Deborah Bowen, Geraldine Shanks, Toshiko Marks, Ian Neary, Roger Goodman, Sue Aylott, Mary Girling and Brenda Corti. Since, unforgivably, I neglected to thank them for their help with previous projects, I would like to take this occasion to say a special thank you to Jane Brooks and Sandra Dyson of the Sir Albert Sloman Library at Essex whose good-humoured indulgence of a wayward borrower has often cheered me up over the past fifteen years.

At a still more practical level, I am happy to acknowledge the financial support provided by the Japan Foundation Endowment Committee and the Contemporary Japan Centre of the University of Essex. In addition I would like to thank the librarians of the Japan Foundation and the Japan Labor Institute in Tokyo for their unfailing friendliness and helpfulness. Under the auspices of the Institute and thanks to its Director, Hirota Osamu, I was also lucky enough to be introduced to Professors Hanami, Kuwahara and Sugeno, all of whom were most helpful, as well as to participate in a programme of factory visits, which was invaluable.

My penultimate debts are threefold: to Gerald Segal for permission to reuse parts of an earlier paper (Woodiwiss 1989) which originally appeared in *Pacific Review*, which he edits; to Berg for permission to use a fragment of my earlier book on labour law in the United States; and finally, as ever, I must thank Kathyanne Hingwan and Frank Pearce for all round support. In particular, I know that I owe a great deal to Kathyanne, who has taught me much as we have shared the pleasures and frustrations of learning about, and living in, Japan. All that remains to be said is the inescapable *mea culpa*.

Tokyo, October 1990

CONVENTIONS

Throughout the book Japanese names appear in the style of that language; that is, surname first and given name second.

INTRODUCTION: THE PROBLEM OF ORIENTALISM AND THE FORMATION OF MODERN JAPAN

Anyone interested in Japanese industrial relations is likely to be struck by a paradox, or the appearance of one. *De facto* Japanese trade unions appear to be rather weak, but *de jure* they seem to be very strong. The principal and interlinked reasons for their *de facto* weakness are usually given as: their enterprise structure, their reluctance to take strike action, and what was until very recently the politically divided nature of their confederations. On the other hand, the principal and again interlinked reasons commonly given for their *de jure* strength are: the constitutionally guaranteed nature of their basic rights and what is normally thought to be the particularly generous nature of the more specific positive laws in which their other rights are defined. The freedom of action, even violent action, which individual Japanese trade unions enjoy on account of their legal position is often supposed to be far greater than that of their 'western' counterparts. Moreover, on this basis they currently organise some 25 per cent of the labour force, which is a far higher percentage than that organised in either France or the United States, for example.

The response of some, especially inside Japan, to the perplexity of others in the face of this contrast is to take it as but further confirmation of a Japanese uniqueness. When misunderstood, this uniqueness causes ethnocentric outsiders to find paradox after paradox in the object of their fascination. I do not agree with this response. Not only do I reject the suggestion that Japan is a unique society, but also I reject the more specific suggestion that the contrast between the *de facto* and *de jure* statuses of Japanese trade unions is anywhere near marked enough to justify being described as a paradox. On the contrary, it seems to me that whilst the observation as to the political–economic weakness of Japanese trade unions is accurate, that as to their legal strength is not.

It is, however, true that in formal legal terms Japanese unions are in some ways less restricted than one might expect given their low level of political–economic clout. They have the Occupation as well as the continuing but still patriarchal and therefore, as I will demonstrate in the main body of this text, highly conditional support of the state to thank for this. However, there is more to legal security, let alone to full social acceptability, than statutes can guarantee and Japanese unions do not possess many of these additional qualities. This is because, first, the Japanese judiciary has proved to be neither particularly interested in defining nor active in up-dating or expanding any rights, let alone those of trade unions. Second, Japan is not a society in which resort to the law is a sign or source of strength. In Japan, therefore, the limits to what the law can provide in the way of enforceable citizenship rights, which according to T. H. Marshall (1962: ch. 4) may be used to ameliorate the inequalities that are otherwise intrinsic to capitalism, are even more restricted than they are in societies where the law is not socially deprecated.

What this study seeks to specify, then, are the nature and sources of these limits as they apply to trade union rights and their use in the pursuit of other rights. For Marshall, the tendency amongst British trade unionists to upgrade their rights from 'civil' to 'political' status, from simple market rights to surrogate political ones, which may then be used in the pursuit of those broader entitlements he termed 'social rights', only remained justifiable as long as what he termed the 'absurd' state of affairs persisted in which unions 'have [still] to bargain for a living wage in a society which accepts the living wage as a social right' (Marshall 1962: 116). If I am more certain than even Marshall would have been that this state of affairs persists today in all of the advanced capitalist societies, it is because I am even more insistent than he was that our conception of 'a living wage' should be a relative one (i.e. relative to a society's general standard of living), as also should be our conception of poverty (cf. Townsend 1979). Thus, *contra* Marshall, what in my view will remain 'impossible' whilst capitalism continues to be the dominant mode of organising economic life, is not the continuation

2

of an 'anomalous' trade union stance, but rather the achievement of a 'living wage' for all and the final eradication of poverty.[1] What, therefore, is as regrettable, in Japan or anywhere else, as any derogation of trade union civil rights, is any reduction of their surrogate political powers. This is because the use of these powers is sometimes necessary for the enforcement of the civil, political and social rights of working people in the face of the ever present, and in Japan especially insistent, demands of duty.

It is undeniable that the use of these powers may on occasion result in serious disruption. This, in turn, may cause some economic, social and even political damage, and of course it plays havoc with the tidy schemes of academics and often falsifies the promises of politicians. Unfortunate as all this un-doubtedly is, it seems to me that, in the absence of a bargained, relatively egalitarian and so-called corporatist settlement of the type to be found in Sweden, the occurrence of any such disrup-tion should be taken as indicating that a meaningful pluralism of values and points of view persists in the societies where it occurs. That is, it indicates that not only do profoundly different views of 'the good society' coexist, but also that labour possesses at least some sanctions with which to support its view. Such sanctions, although they may be mobilised only occasionally and always with great difficulty, provide labour with a modi-cum of countervailing power upon which to draw in the face of that which is otherwise intrinsic to capital's social position. The latter powers are those which tend to identify capital with that dutiful 'quiet life', which is sometimes confused with 'the good life'. In what follows I will argue that Japanese labour lacks access to such sanctions and that the law, which is supposedly so generous to labour, has played an important role in confirm-ing this lack. What I have written, therefore, should be read as a cautionary tale, not only by those who are concerned about the consequences of the export of Japanese production facilities and management strategies for trade union rights in the importing countries, but also by those who take the currently fashionable position that the mere strengthening of citizenship rights is sufficient to ensure the continuation of social progress in ad-vanced capitalist societies (see Hall and Jacques 1989). The rise of fascism in Europe during the interwar period demonstrated how vulnerable such rights are to political pre-emption, whilst what the postwar history of Japanese labour law demonstrates is how vulnerable they are to ideological pre-emption, even in democratic societies.

In sum, what will be attempted here is the dissolution of a paradox not the explication of one. This attempt will proceed at two levels. On one level, the fact of Japanese trade unions' legal weakness with respect to their civil rights will be established for each of the three periods into which modern Japanese history is conventionally divided. On the other level, and with respect to the same historical periods, this weakness will be explained as being in large part a simple corollary of the weakness of the law as a means of enforcing such rights in Japan, as well as of the weakness, again for Japan-specific social–structural reasons, of any Marshallian, surrogate political powers on the part of trade unions. The study will end by drawing three sets of conclusions. The first will involve making an assessment of the current strength and possible future significance of Japanese trade unions. The second will be concerned to provide an explanation for the absence from Japan of that 'secondary industrial citizenship', which Marshall (1962: 116) regarded as the consequence of trade union civil rights becoming surrogate political ones. The third will specify the significance of the first two for what seems to me to be the highly germane debate as to whether or not Japan is a postmodern society (Miyoshi and Harootunian 1989).

Before any of this is attempted, however, and as an essential preliminary, some attention must first be paid to the more general issue of Japan's supposed uniqueness and its bearing on how the society's entry into the 'modern' era should be conceptualised.

A UNIQUE SOCIETY?

Over the past few years two Australia-based social scientists, Sugimoto Yoshio and Ross Mouer (1984), have made particularly strenuous efforts to clarify the problems encountered by comparativists, such as myself, when we turn our attention to Japan.[2] All of us are very much in their debt. This said, their proposed method of resolving these problems will not be followed here. They touch on what I have already implied is the fundamental problem with the existing literature – the extremely widespread assumption that Japan is, as Sugimoto and Mouer put it, 'uniquely unique' and that for this reason it may not be properly understood by 'western' social science. However, their mode of argumentation is such that they never fully get to critical grips with this assumption. Indeed their proposed means of overcoming the problems it has bequeathed rests, contradictorily, on the assumption's maintenance: for them every society is unique, but none are uniquely unique.

Their argument proceeds by means of a typology of works on Japan which presents them as dependent upon either a 'consensus model' or a 'conflict model' and concludes with an argument for the superiority of the latter. The difficulty here is not simply that their typology is somewhat antiquated and that many of their classifications are rather forced, but more significantly that the assumption of uniqueness is common to instances of both models. Since I wish to be very clearly understood to reject this assumption, I will proceed in a rather different way. This way is premissed upon the principle that all societies are different, but none are unique. More specifically, it finds the origin of our problems in understanding Japan not in some failure to appreciate its uniqueness, but rather in a fault in the manner in which until recently Japan has been constituted as an object of study in the social sciences. This approach involves no less of a radical departure from the orthodoxies of the western social scientific heritage than the former, but it has none of its regrettable consequences. Specifically, what I wish to emphasise is the important but in this instance very unfortunate role played by what Hayden White (1973) has called historiographical 'poetics' in the process whereby the objects of social scientific knowledge are constituted. For this reason the latter part of this introduction will indicate the critical bearing that recent scholarship has had on the hitherto well-established representation of the founding event of modern Japan, the Meiji Restoration, as a paradox: an uprising inspired by a highly traditional ideology which nevertheless ushered in a period of rapid and radical social change. Thus the two principal questions addressed in the remainder of this introduction are as follows. In what ways does the trope of paradox protect the assumption as to Japan's uniqueness? How can we avoid working with such an assumption and still understand Japan's particularity?

ORIENTALISM

The reasons why the uniqueness assumption should be rejected are twofold; first, it owes its existence to the intellectual dominance of a pernicious, quasi-academic discourse which, following Edward Said (1979), we have learnt to call 'orientalism'. Second, and as a consequence, it calls into question, for no good reason, the applicability of the social sciences to the Japanese case. According to this discourse, Japan, like all the other societies of what in the eighteenth and nineteenth centuries was constructed as 'the east', is not simply different from or even opposite to 'the west', but also its 'other' and usually its inferior (see also Minear 1980). Additionally, because of Japan's intentional two hundred years of 'seclusion' (i.e. conscious rejection of 'the west') the society was and still is often thought to be not merely enigmatic but enticingly or threateningly so. This, of course, makes it deeply ironic that, as will become clear in the main text, those who today most strongly champion the uniqueness assumption's social scientific claims are nationalistically inclined Japanese academics. Less surprising is the recent emergence of a body of 'revisionist' western literature which is so insistent that Japan *is* different that it is difficult to distinguish between their position and that of those who claim that it is unique (see especially van Wolferen 1989). Additionally and more pertinently in the present context, the pervasiveness of orientalism perhaps also explains why non-Japanese scholars have been generally so unresisting to the idea that modern Japan's foundational event was a paradoxical one. The figure of paradox provides a means of preserving a preference for, or a suspicion of, Japan's otherness in the face of its increasing likeness – 'something happened in the course of the Meiji Restoration that we do not fully understand and which may yet turn out to have unexpected consequences' seems to be the ever present subtext.

ORIENTALISM AND NATIONALISM IN JAPAN

For reasons that have been best explained by Michel Foucault (e.g. 1970; 1979), even the most tired of academic clichés may remain in general circulation, and indeed re-enter academic discourse itself, provided only, to put it very simply, that they constitute, and so in this special sense serve, some powerful

6

interest. Thus my suggestion is that the idea of Japan's uniqueness persists in certain quarters of Japanese academia because it is part of the bedrock of Japanese nationalism. And so as long as, for example, the society remains economically successful and this success is thought (by sympathetic as well as critical 'westerners' too) to be the product of specifically Japanese institutional forms (e.g. The *Japanese* Employment System) and/or cultural characteristics; and as long as the Liberal Democratic Party (LDP) rests its appeal on being the party that most effectively nurtures these characteristics, the idea of Japan's uniqueness will retain its place as a central term in the vocabulary that the society's members have available for understanding themselves (see pp. 85–91).

It is not surprising therefore that the recent upsurge in the popular literature on 'Japaneseness' (*Nihonjinron*) in Japan should have coincided with the intensification of what is euphemistically known as 'the trade friction' with the United States. Whilst it may have been understandable, even within the terms of a nationalist discourse, that the United States should have so forcefully rejected 'the *Yamato* (aboriginal Japanese) spirit' when it was expressed militarily during the course of the Second World War, it is very hard for some Japanese to understand when today's pacific, economic advance is also so forcefully rejected. The difference is that in this case it is widely agreed within Japan that there is no reason why this injured spirit should not be nursed back to health again. In this way, then, the idea of Japan's uniqueness persists, accompanied by its nationalist connotations. It remains available for deployment not just in popular or political discourses but also, as will be made plain in the main body of the present text, in those of academia and the law too (see Woodiwiss 1989: 39–41).

THE RESTORATION AS A PARADOX

There are by now numerous studies that in one way or another expose the 'sordid little crimes' surrounding the birth and much of the subsequent life of the social sciences, including those aspects of them that relate to Japan (e.g. Dower 1975: introduction; Sugimoto and Mouer 1984). Many Japanese social scientists have struggled, and I use the term advisedly, as hard or harder with the baleful consequences of these little crimes than have their 'western' counterparts. Here I am thinking particularly of the Rono and Koza factions within Japanese academic Marxism, whose brave thoughts, disputes and suffering during the 1930s and 1940s have recently, and at last, been so well chronicled for English-speaking readers by Germaine Hoston (1986). I will now indicate some of their differences before specifying the significance of the debate they launched for the representation of the Meiji Restoration as a paradox and, by extension, for that which is thereby protected, namely the assumption that Japan is a unique society.

Until recently 'the paradox formula' more or less completely dominated Restoration scholarship, even when, as was frequent, one or other of its terms was rejected. For the Koza faction and also for some ultra-conservative nationalist writers of the 1930s, it was the notion of radical, post-Restoration social change that was rejected, since for them traditionalist ideology remained too strong to have allowed any such change, as was apparently confirmed by the then rising tide of militarism. (For a development of the Marxist version of this argument see Jon Halliday's sadly underdiscussed *A Political History of Japanese Capitalism* 1976). By contrast, for the Rono faction and later for the primarily American, modernisation theorists of the 1950s and 1960s it was the notion that the Restoration's ideological inspiration was either entirely traditional or even particularly influential, given the arrival of capitalism and 'western learning', that had to be rejected, since its results, the 'aberration' of militarism excepted, seemed to them to have been so progressive. What is striking is that throughout this whole body of literature, of which Nakane Chie's much referenced if regrettably undercriticised *Japanese Society* (Nakane 1970) is the totemic centrepiece, the idea of Japan's uniqueness retains its place, whether it is understood to account for benign or malign developments.

More recently, although its possibility was glimpsed percipiently in the 1940s by E. H. Norman (whose suicide and subsequent scholarly neglect is one of the not so little crimes associated with postwar Japanese Studies), another strategy for dealing with the paradox has become apparent, as scholars have tried to come to terms with some of the more awkward facts that monographic studies have produced: for example, concerning the possibilities inherent in 'Taisho democracy' and the absence of uniform poverty amongst the prewar peasantry. This strategy involves continuing to accept the paradox whilst attempting to soften the antinomy that lies at its heart. Thus the concept of Restoration has been broadened, the period of time to which it refers has been lengthened and 'restoratory' and 'renovatory' phases or dimensions have been distinguished within it (e.g. Beasley 1972). But still the assumption as to Japan's uniqueness is not challenged directly in this literature. However, further awkward facts, especially about the diversity of pre-Meiji thought, may be found in this literature and these have turned out to have a latently subversive significance for the assumption, as became manifest in Harry Harootunian's *Toward Restoration* (1970).

THE RESTORATION WITHOUT PARADOX

As a result of mulling over the empirical legacy as well as over his own findings, and inspired by a body of theory in which certain Marxist and what are now called 'postmodernist' ideas were combined, Harootunian challenged the applicability of the trope of paradox as applied to the Restoration. In so doing he opened the way to as yet largely unwritten histories of and social scientific works on many other aspects of Japanese society that do not depend on what Peter Dale (1988) has recently and entirely appropriately termed 'the myth of Japanese uniqueness'. Harootunian's thesis is best introduced by quoting from the conclusion to his first book:

> While they appealed widely to 'tradition', by 1867 there was no agreement at all on what constituted the inherited tradition. I would argue that the appeal to tradition was simply a device to promote schemes that were not traditional at all. This technique is clearest in the metaphor of restoration itself. Because men had long been calling for a repudiation of the past to ensure a proper commitment to the present, the restorers resorted to native mytho-history to express the newness of their effort.
>
> (Harootunian 1970: 404)

Since this was written, Harootunian has elaborated on this insight and on his suggestion that the source of the dynamism within late Tokugawa thought was the contrast between the conservatism of Restorationist ideology and 'the rage' of its 'activist' proponents (cf. Najita 1974). Now, following Foucault, he sees the source of this dynamism in more strictly sociological terms as the consequence of the appearance of a new and in part individualistic epistemological discourse which stood in a relation of irrepressible tension with the received Confucian 'Way' of knowledge. This tension had what ultimately proved to be very radical social consequences as it interacted with ongoing and apparently unconnected political and economic changes, such as the sharpening of *'han'* (clan) rivalries, *tozama* (outer lords)/*bakufu* (shogunate) tensions, the gradual dissolution of the feudal economy and the emergence of capitalism. These consequences he exemplifies by reference to the emergence of Mito scholarship, an indigenous, individualistic political economy, and nativist as well as 'new' religious social movements. All of these exhibited strong secessionist tendencies in relation to the Shogunate and thus exacerbated the problems it faced, since they sought new forms of social order, which significantly (*contra* Nakane and others) were characterised by the presence within them of strong 'horizonealist' (i.e. anti-hierarchical) elements (Harootunian 1982).

What, in turn, makes all of this subversive of the myth of uniqueness is not so much the similarity of the 'rumour of revolutionary energy' (Harootunian 1982: 45) involved to that which was present in Europe at around the same time, but rather its corrosive consequences for the trope of paradox. If Restorationist ideology was not a unity, then it could not have been informed by a single essence or expressive of a single spirit, *yamato* or otherwise. Thus Japan did not undergo the transition from feudalism to capitalism in any unique way, guided by any uniquely unitary or uniquely defined traditionalist ideology. On the contrary it underwent this transition to the accompaniment of what was in many ways a fundamentally similar (how else could 'western learning' have been assimilated?), if rather differently inflected, range of ideas and so without paradox although very definitely not without tensions. But, again, these were the same tensions – pre-eminently between labour and agricultural capital – as were present in Europe. The fact that these were ideologically materialised in a very different way is as undeniable as it was inevitable and ought no longer to cause us to find mysteries where there are only challenges to research.

And it is to the meeting of one of these challenges, the understanding of the development of Japanese labour law, that this text will now turn.

A SOCIOLOGICAL APPROACH TO THE HISTORY OF LABOUR LAW: CONCEPTS AND QUESTIONS

Unconstrained by 'the myth of uniqueness' and drawing on the same body of Marxist and post-structuralist theory as Harootunian, the same theories of law and class may be depended upon and the same three substantive questions posed here in relation to Japan as have been posed elsewhere in relation to the development of labour law in the United States.

To repeat more or less verbatim what I have written in these other places (principally, Woodiwiss 1990a: 9–10; 1990b: 115–16), the theory of law upon which I depend is broadly Marxist. However, it involves a rejection of one of the central substantive tenets of traditional Marxist theory, namely the belief that the law in capitalist societies is irremediably an instrument for the protection of capitalist private property. Rather, it argues that, like the state (Jessop 1982), the law in democratic capitalist societies is characterised by a certain autonomy in the relations between it and the class structure. A relative autonomy that is understood, in a Foucauldian (1974) sense, to inhere in the particularities of its discourse.

Although the law is primarily and self-evidently an instance of discourse, it has taken an inordinately long time for it to be recognised as such by legal theorists. Rather, they have tended, and indeed still tend, to divide over from whom or from what does the law issue: is it from god, nature, the sovereign, the ruling class, politicians or judges? As a result the law itself has been consistently denied what seems to me to be its proper, determinative role in accounts of even its *own* historical development. Thus its powers have been too often reduced to those of its authors and/or enunciators.

In any event, it seems to me that only once one is prepared to grant the law the autonomy which is inherent in its nature as in part a discourse does it become possible to explain why and how what is generally the fair application of the law nevertheless only sometimes favours the subject classes, whilst it generally favours the dominant ones. Given such an acknowledgement, capitalist

11

law may be defined in morphological terms as: a set of state-enunciated and enforced discourses which interpellates the subjects it addresses in such a way that they will be law-abiding, provided that the same subjects do not successfully resist this disciplining because of prior or other interpellations originating in and/or articulated with counter-discourses.

The principal means by which, when so understood, the law may be understood to affect the wider society are twofold. First, the law produces a background 'ideology-effect' in that, provided it is universalistically applied and fairly administered, it reinforces and so helps to maintain the patterns of social relationships that comprise the social formation of which it is a part. Second, and more innovatively within the Marxist tradition, once the law is understood as a set of discourses it is possible to specify the means whereby law produces this 'ideology-effect' in capitalist societies; i.e. by intermittently and, in the normal course of events, irresistibly reordering the relational balances known to it in terms of rights and duties on the basis of a discursive practice whose guiding methodological principle is 'consistency'.

The foundational and constitutive role of 'consistency' in capitalist law is what gives legal discourse its autonomy. However, 'consistency' is never a self-subsisting sign in legal or in any other form of discourse. It must always be articulated with other signs which signify a substantive rather than a methodological principle before it can mean anything – e.g. 'liberty', 'equality' and, especially in the Japanese case, 'patriarchy' in their multiple meanings and combinations. Thus, whether or not any substantive as opposed to merely formal consistency exists and so whether or not the law operates to the benefit of labour will vary, and vary quite markedly, according to the more general ideological background with which any such substantive principle is necessarily imbricated. In sum, it is the necessity of the articulation of 'consistency' with substantive principles and of these principles with wider ideological discourses which ensures that the autonomy of law in capitalist societies is always relative – relative to a particular social structure and thus generally but not solely to the particular extra-legal discourses enunciated by those who are the most powerful and/or the most frequent users of the law.

If what differentiates my theory of capitalist law from that to be found in more orthodox Marxist texts is its rejection of the latter's economic reductionism, then the same may also be said of the theory of class with which I work (Woodiwiss 1990b: pt IV). However, what is still more distinctive about my approach to class is that it is premissed upon the view that in taking individuals and/or groups as the units of class analysis most previous theories (Marxist as well as Weberian) have been mistaken. In my view, to attempt to construct sociological categories by trying to draw lines around groups of people is to embark upon a mistaken and anyway impossible task (*vide* the proliferating intermediary sub-classes to be found within the class schema of the likes of John Goldthorpe 1980 and Erik Olin Wright 1985).

It seems to me that individual people are always too unpredictable to be ever usefully categorised in this way and so provide any sort of firm basis for sociological reasoning. This unpredictability may only be elucidated by recourse to psychology. Thus instead of pursuing this impossible and mistaken end and in order that it may also contribute something of its own to the elucidation of this unpredictability, sociology should follow Durkheim's advice and concern itself with discovering, and making its analyses in terms of, entities that are social in a *sui generis* sense.

This at least is what I have attempted to do in my effort to continue the work commenced, but later abandoned, by Althusser, Poulantzas and Hindess and Hirst, namely the effort to rethink Marx's class theory on a non-humanist basis. For me, the classes of capitalist societies are not in the first instance collectivities of people but rather things in their own right, ensembles of economic, political and ideological structural positions, which are held together by the forces produced by capital's appropriation of surplus labour. Classes as things are, of course, in part embodied by people and corporate entities, but not necessarily by them as whole entities. Thus in some of their beliefs and behaviours, and whether they are acting inside or outside of the sphere of production, both people and corporate institutions such as companies and trade unions may embody capital whilst in others of their beliefs and behaviours they may also embody the working class. Finally, in the absence of additional modes of production, there are only two classes in capitalist societies – the capitalist and the working classes.

The intrinsic structural tensions and therefore the nature of the continuing, reciprocally structuring effects of the two classes upon one another and upon the boundary between them will vary from social formation to social formation, because, of course, the particular economic, political and ideological structures upon which classes osmotically depend also vary, as also do the ongoing relatively autonomous developmental dynamics of these structures. Moreover, similarly varying are the additional, abstractly supernumerary, but concretely usually superincumbent osmotic processes (those relating to 'race' and gender, for example) which may come to structure concrete production relations in particular societies. The former set of variations may lead to varying forms and degrees of segmentation within classes and fractionalisation amongst their embodiments. Similarly, the latter set may lead either to classes as a whole or to particular segments of them being overlain and hence additionally affected by economic, political or ideological positions that are not intrinsically pertinent to the appropriation of surplus labour. Nevertheless these superincumbent positions will almost always affect if not the structure of classes themselves then their social effects by the additional constraints they impose on the nature of the subjects that can embody particular sets or sub-sets of class positionings (a requirement, for example, that the embodiment of skilled labour power in a large manufacturing enterprise should be a non-*burakumin* (untouchable) Japanese male, with a high school diploma). Thus, concrete classes and, as will become apparent below, the effects of the tensions between them are likely to be marked and affected by such factors as levels of technological development, international and domestic market conditions and a whole range of political and ideological conditions which might otherwise be thought of as entirely unrelated to class relations.

The net result of this approach is that one need no longer think, as the hitherto theoretically determinant humanist metaphor of 'class struggle' has for so long directed, in terms of two or more armies confronting one another in an 'arena' or on a field ('terrain'). Rather, one may think of the class structure of capitalist society as a structural unity which is divided into two and sometimes segmented as a necessary consequence of the relations that constitute it as a whole. And the boundary between these two classes, populated by the contradictorily positioned but in no way corporate 'middle classes', will gain or lose definition as a consequence of changes in its constitutive relations.

The import of all of this for the understanding of the social significance of labour law is that it changes the nature of the questions one asks. Specifically, as a sociologist rather than as a politician or, perhaps, rather than as a political scientist, one should no longer ask questions directly about the effects of labour law on the size, internal organisation and morale of a supposed working-class 'army' (the traditional Marxist and Weberian questions). Rather, one should ask questions about the affect of labour law on the strength of the forces that bind and separate the two classes economically, politically and ideologically, and which therefore explain the ease or difficulty of capital's appropriation of surplus labour.

In sum, one should ask questions about the affect of labour law on: (1) capital's economic possession of its property in the means of production (i.e. on labour market conditions); (2) capital's political or disciplinary control of the productive process (i.e. on disciplinary conditions); and (3) capital's ideological right of title (i.e. on the significatory conditions which pertain to its claim to any profits which arise from its operations). Necessarily, these are also questions about the balance of forces between labour and capital.

The mere posing of these questions immediately makes it clear why most often any affect that labour law, if not any trade unions empowered by it, may have upon class relations is unlikely to be dramatic. This is because, as will be amply demonstrated in the case study which follows, except where it establishes 'co-determination' structures which allow labour some power of control (as in Germany), or where it establishes what might be termed 'title-sharing' arrangements (as exemplified by Sweden's Wage-Earner Funds), the effects of labour law are generally confined to possessory relations alone. To conclude, only after the elaborate structural analysis just outlined has been completed is one in any position to consider and attempt to elucidate the responses of individual and collective subjects to the forces amidst which and in terms of which they live.[3]

Three substantive historical questions are prompted by the theoretical considerations just outlined. These are: (1) Why and

15

under what circumstances did the law enter industrial relations at particular points in time? (2) How was it that particular legal interventions had the outcomes they did? (3) What were the effects of these outcomes on the conditions which gave rise to the initial interventions? The first question may be answered by reference to the changing political, ideological and economic conditions and/or the changing class relations pertaining to industrial relations, and which on occasion have resulted either in legal changes or in one or other party going to law when they previously would not have done. The second question may be answered by reference to the specific legal incidents themselves. Here, two aspects should be investigated: the precise nature of the interventions attempted and the structure of the pertinent legal discourses. Finally, the third question may be answered on the basis of a consideration of the following complex of factors: the balance of disciplinary or political forces obtaining in the pertinent economic/industrial sites; the consequences of particular resorts to the law for these disciplinary balances; and, finally, the consequences of any changes in the discursive structure of labour law for the conditions which initially gave rise to the interventions, especially as these are mediated through the class and other social structures. Of course, the answers to the second and third questions may derive from the first. However, they need not, and the purpose of keeping the three questions separate is both to allow for this, and to facilitate the acknowledgement of particular, autonomous forces at the discursive or disciplinary levels and their varying relations of determination. In sum, the point is that the development of labour law may only be fully understood if specific discursive and/or disciplinary struggles and developments are taken into account as well as the more general social–structural ones.

THE DEVELOPMENT OF JAPANESE LABOUR LAW

The doyen of British labour lawyers, Otto Kahn-Freund (1977), suggested that three phases may be distinguished within the histories of most labour law systems: one of 'repression', one of 'toleration' and one of 'recognition'. Of course, he also recognised that the legal realities pertaining to any particular history seldom lend themselves to quite such a neat periodisation (for a survey of the histories of nine major European societies, see

Hepple 1986; and for the American case, see Woodiwiss 1990a).
The principal point of difference between Japanese labour law's
trajectory and Kahn-Freund's ideal-type is the absence from it
of an at all substantial phase of toleration, even one that could
be characterised, like that which occurred in the United States,
as one of 'reluctant toleration'. Until 1945, independent trade
unions were repressed because they were regarded as alien to
the *kokutai* (the imperial Japanese polity). Their belated recognition in 1945 was a consequence of the industrial and social
disorganisation of the early postwar years, as well as of the
unions' initial centrality to the Occupation's programme of reform. In other words, rather than being the product of a gradual
process of union self-assertion and societal accommodation, the
recognition of unions was imposed upon Japanese capital within a social–structural environment which had been and has
remained very resistant to them. The result is that union recognition was and still is conjoined with a profound reluctance
which has in fact intensified since the early 1970s. Thus my
substantive aims in what follows will be: first, to explain why
the social structure was so resistant to unions in the prewar
period; second, to assess and explain the significance of this
heritage for Japan's contemporary system of labour law, especially as it relates to the legislative inhibition of any assumption
by trade unions of any Marshallian, surrogate political powers;
third, to specify and explain the role of judicial decisions in the
tightening of these and other constraints on unions since the
early 1970s; and fourth, to draw some specific conclusions as to
how any future laws or amendments which might seek to enact
or strengthen citizenship rights should be drafted so as to ensure
that they do in fact have such results.

NOTES

1 For a summary and discussion of, as well as an important contribution to, the complex and extensive debate on the wider issue of
   'capitalism and citizenship', see Turner 1986.
2 The remainder of the discussion of this issue is largely an adapted
   and edited version of a section of Woodiwiss 1989.
3 This is all that will be said here concerning theory. Readers requiring
   further theoretical elucidation are recommended to consult
   Woodiwiss 1990b, especially parts III and IV. Otherwise, or where
   the reader has no interest in theory, I am content that what follows

should be judged on the basis of its empirical and explanatory plausibility.

Part I

PREWAR SOCIETY AND THE REPRESSION OF LABOUR

1

EARLY MEIJI SOCIETY AND THE ABSENCE OF LABOUR LAW

One important reason why the notion that Japan's trade unions enjoy a strong legal position is so widespread is because virtually all past discussions of the issue have begun with the Occupation and the passage of the legislation now in force. Irrespective of whether it was made consciously or unconsciously, such a choice of starting point implies a view that the Occupation represented a far more radical social transformation than is acceptable here. The Occupation changed many things that are pertinent to the present discussion, most obviously the Constitution and the nature of the more specific positive law governing industrial relations. Taken literally, these changes benefited labour immensely. However, taking things literally does not or should not come easily to social scientists. They know that positive law does not exclusively determine either what is socially enforced or even sometimes what is legally enforceable.

As Kahn-Freund argues in *Labour and the Law*, the law is 'a secondary force in human affairs' (1977). By this he means that it cannot force itself on society and, as a corollary, that its importance in any particular society is determined by social processes other than that which it represents itself. In other words, the social importance of the law may vary greatly from society to society and even within one society over time. Modern Japan always has been and still is a society in which the law is relatively unimportant. However, the proximate causes of this unimportance have changed markedly over the years. In the course of a discussion of what might best be called 'the underdevelopment' of labour law, the first part of this book will specify the changing causes of this unimportance during the

21

prewar period. Knowledge of this pre-history is essential if the otherwise common judgement as to the current strength of Japanese labour's legal position is to be reversed.

The whole of the period 1868–1945 may be treated as a unity. Labour law, as a developed discourse of rights and duties in the workplace, was notable by its absence throughout this period. In so far as it existed, it remained largely a matter of the criminal law and police repression. However, the reasons for this state of affairs changed over time and so for analytical convenience the period will be divided into two: the early Meiji period (1868–89) and the period during which the Meiji Constitution was in force (1889–1945).

THE FORMATION OF THE EARLY MEIJI STATE

Although the Restoration was a product of economic and ideological as well as political changes, it was in itself essentially a political event. This section will begin, therefore, with a discussion of the structure of the Meiji state. Indeed if one does not so begin, it is hard to know how to divide up any account of the development of modern Japan. The changes in the other spheres were gradual, uneven, and anyway always very clearly overdetermined by political changes. Most pertinently, if one does not appreciate how slowly the changes in the other spheres followed those in politics, it is hard to explain why labour law's arrival was so long delayed, as well as why it took such an attenuated form when it did eventually appear.

The early Meiji state was not a *Rechtsstaat* (law state) since its citizenry were subject to no unitary and universally applicable set of laws (Henderson 1968a: 415). It was instead a variant of the absolutist state, as scholars in the Marxist tradition have long maintained (e.g. Norman 1940). However, although non-Marxist scholars have been singularly loath to acknowledge it, neither the Japanese Marxist tradition nor Norman in particular intended to suggest by their use of the term what had traditionally been suggested by their European Marxist colleagues; namely, that as an absolutism the early Meiji state was necessarily antipathetic to capitalist development. Indeed the disagreement between the Koza and Rono factions, from which Norman learnt a great deal, was very much concerned with this issue and the Rono faction took a position opposed to the European orthodoxy (Hoston 1987).

In Europe today, although many Marxist scholars persist with the traditional view (e.g. Anderson 1974), some others, notably Hindess and Hirst (1975) and Lublinskaya (1968), have adopted a position closer to the Rona one and indeed to that of the non-Marxist historians of 'enlightened despotism'. According to this position, absolutist states are understood to be the products of feudal conflicts and yet to be capable of acting in ways favourable to capitalist development without themselves being properly capitalist states.[1]

The identification of the pre-*Rechtsstaat*, Meiji state as absolutist in the sense specified here enables one to make four statements about it. First, that it was an example of a far from unique state form which had no inherent relationship – pro or con – to capitalism. Second, that it was constructed in the midst of, or as in this case (and in this regard it was distinctive) in the aftermath of, what proved to be a terminal explosion of feudal conflicts. Third, that it was a state whose significance for capitalist development was dependent upon the balance of economic, political and ideological forces that supported it. And fourth, that it was a state wherein power was centralised in a monarchy possessed of a bureaucratic apparatus, which the occupant of the throne personally controlled, if in many respects only nominally.

The second of these statements requires some discussion, since it indicates a substantive divergence between the present position and that to be found in Norman (1940) and Japanese Marxism (see also Halliday 1976). Specifically, the present author does not share his predecessors' insistence on the critical importance of capitalist development and especially of capitalist merchants in the crisis that finally saw the collapse of the Tokugawa shogunate. I do not dispute capitalism's existence in late Tokugawa Japan, nor indeed the importance of the external pressures represented by 'western capitalism', which Norman emphasises, but only, like most non-Marxist historians (e.g. Craig 1961), their centrality to the Restoration crisis itself.

The import of this divergence is that, since neither any particular capitalists nor capitalism in general (*contra* Anderson 1974: 435 ff.) may be understood to have emerged as victors from the Restoration conflicts, their subsequent rapid advance is something that has to be explained rather than assumed as is otherwise most often the case on both sides of the historiographical divide.[2] Indeed it will be suggested below that the only basis upon which it is possible to understand why it required a military defeat and foreign occupation before the state withdrew from direct intervention in the workplace, is if one refuses the proposition that the interests of the prewar state were exclusively or even primarily identified with those of capital. Throughout the sub-period presently under discussion, the state and capital shared some interests. Each was a highly significant condition of the other's existence and so some complementarity was inevitable. However, their relationship was characterised by a striking degree of 'relative autonomy'. This was the consequence of the fact that Meiji absolutism was established after the collapse of feudalism, but before capitalism obtained even economic dominance; i.e. the early Meiji state enjoyed an unusual degree of freedom from economic constraints of a structural, even if not of a fiscal, kind.

THE EARLY MEIJI STATE

What, then, were the characteristics of the early Meiji social formation that allowed this unusual degree of state autonomy? And what, to begin with, were the characteristics of the state itself? The first thing that has to be said about this state is something which takes us to the heart of the issues that relate to its autonomy. It is that, for the most part, and to a far greater degree than its European equivalents, it was a new structure. Not only did the process of state-creation directly impose a particular 'logic' (Jessop 1987) on and thereby constrain the actions of state incumbents, but it also overlay and in this way shaped and constrained other structures and actors. State-creation, then, was the principal source of the state's autonomous concerns.

One element of the state, however, was not new. This was, of course, the position of *tenno* (emperor), since the call for its restoration to primacy within the state was what had legitimated all the pre-Restoration strife. However, what was expected of the position in the new conditions was very different from that which had been expected hitherto. It had to become, in Bagehot's terms, an 'efficient' as well as a 'dignified' part of the state. 'How

24

could or should this happen?' is a question that appears to have preoccupied *tenno* Meiji and the oligarchs who ruled with him, especially the seven or so *genro* (elder statesmen). After an initial dalliance with liberalistic, Anglo–American notions in the Charter Oath and the Constitution, both of 1868, the state-makers appear to have moved uncertainly but steadily away from such ideas and especially their connotations of popular sovereignty and representation. The details are not as important as the fact that the net result of their deliberations, prior to the establishment of a *Rechtsstaat*, was the absolutist state that has already been briefly discussed. It was constructed as a result of a great deal of trial, error and intrigue, within which ideological disputation played little direct part. For this reason, its coordination and staffing were marked by a distinctive and overwhelming concern with personal loyalty (Ishii 1980: ch.5; McLaren 1965; Silberman 1982). The latter is a fact of some significance in the light of the emerging themes of *tennosei* (emperor system) ideology, as will become apparent below.

In the absence of an explicit commitment to capitalism on the part of the state-makers, and in the context of a continuing fear of resurgent feudal forces, which only receded after the crushing of the Satsuma rebellion of 1877, the exigencies of state-making seem to explain better the decisions that are otherwise most often cited as indicative of the state's commitment to capitalism. The final destruction of feudalism, including such of its incidents as the system of landholding, *han* and *samurai* privileges, and merchant and artisanal guilds, was not so much a forward-looking policy decision as an attempt to secure the conditions of the new state's very existence in what Umegaki (1988) has emphasised were the rather fraught conditions that persisted for some ten years or so after the Restoration. Thus Japan became capitalist almost by default. To use a well-known Gramscian phrase, it witnessed a most passive of 'passive revolutions'. The positive measures undertaken by the state, including the establishment of private property in land, were considered necessary for primarily fiscal and security reasons, as even Norman (1940: 136–43) recognised. Without them the new state would have possessed neither the secure and dependable revenues nor the monopoly over legitimate force that, since Weber, have been understood as the prerequisites of any state's existence. Similarly, the formation of the new conscript army, the creation of a police force, the pursuit of 'western learning', the improvement of domestic communications and the establishment of state-owned factories, are all readily understandable when located in the same context and seen as a response to the same exigencies of state-making.

Of course, each of these developments was highly propitious from the point of view of capital. But that is all they were – promising not promises. In any event, capital was too weak to have possessed the means necessary either to extract or to enforce any such promises. (The qualified nature of the ideologically critical protection of private property will be specified below.) This said, the developments very definitely were propitious and not just as messages from the Shinto *kami* (ancestral spirits). The latter were themselves being reinvigorated and, like the *tenno*-state that they were about to inhabit, their aggrandisement was the main concern of their servants. Moreover, the latter activity also proved to be propitious from capital's point of view, and for a similar reason. Accidental as both sets of benificences were, the *Kokutai* thus constructed was to so structure the environment of production that, and especially in the absence of any viable or, better, equally clearly and powerfully articulated challenges, capital profited mightily from it both nationally and in the workplace. However, in relation to the period presently under discussion the benefits of these effects were still largely in the future. Few were the enterprises that were capable of profiting immediately from the new economic freedoms: large-scale enterprises barely existed and the very numerous, small, simple commodity producing ones were only very slowly reconstituting themselves on the basis of capitalist relations of production.

In short, because of its particular conditions of existence, the early Meiji state, as a set of institutions and administrative routines, so constrained the actions of its incumbents that their actions became subject to an overwhelming logic of state-creation. This meshed with that operative within the capitalist sector of the economy in ways that were often only accidentally or tangentially complementary and were sometimes even anti-pathetic (Akita 1967: 165 ff.). The autonomy so gained, although it became somewhat more relative in the sense of somewhat more constrained by the demands of capital, was never greatly threatened in the pre–1945 period. This was because, with the partial exception of those industrialists who read the earlier works of Fukuzawa, *the* liberal thinker of the Meiji era, very few had much sense, ideologically, of their special needs (Marshall 1967). Nor, as it turned out, was it economically necessary that they should have any such sense.

THE CREATION OF A CAPITALIST ECONOMY

In the literature pertaining to the economic history of late Tokugawa and early Meiji Japan, there is general agreement that capitalist production relations existed and were of some significance within the economy.[3] However, the analytical criteria upon which such judgements are based are seldom made explicit. In so far as they are, they often seem to be in conflict with the descriptions that are offered of the relations concerned. More specifically, emphasis is placed on aspects of exchange rather than production: on the emergence of a money economy; on the consequent monetisation of agricultural relationships; on the growth of a rural/urban artisanate; and on the growing importance of urban merchants (*shonin*) in terms of their wealth, the financial dependence of many feudal lords on them and their ownership of reclaimed land (i.e. *shinden*, or land 'unknown' to the shogunal authorities, Nakamura 1983: 49). In these ways capitalism is said to have established itself.

When, however, one reads descriptions of the production relations obtaining within the productive units so circumscribed (e.g. Hirschmeier and Yui 1981; Smith 1959), one is struck by their similarity to those generally classified as instances of simple commodity production. They are those, in other words, that normally would be recognised as father/family, or master/servant relations, wherein the powers intrinsic to possession are vested in the head of the 'house' or *ie* (household). The major difference between them and their European equivalents would seem to have been that aspects of their conditions of existence radically reduced the autonomy of the 'houses' relative to feudalism, as well as reduced, therefore, the possibility of their being transmuted into resilient capitalist enterprises. For example, agricultural landholdings, merchant ownership of buildings and the land upon which they stood, reclaimed land, and the commodities in which they dealt, all seem to have been secure enough (see p.34). However, the existence of both lordly prerogatives and variable tax/rent levels always influenced and could have been used to determine the productivity of, and so to assert a lordly possessory power over, agriculture, although it appears they seldom were. Nevertheless, loans could be and often were forced from merchants by the *daimyo* (feudal lords), who seldom felt under any obligation to repay them. Additionally, restrictions on the free movement of labour were rigorously enforced. And finally, possessory rights were legitimated by an uncompromisingly feudal ideology, which made the enjoyment of any such rights very dependent upon the goodwill of social superiors. In the case of the merchants, this included virtually everyone else, even their employees, the landless peasantry.

All that said, there seems to be no reason to doubt that many artisans, merchants and other non-lordly property holders nevertheless not only sustained their autonomy as simple commodity producers, but also succeeded in transforming their 'houses' and farms into capitalist enterprises, albeit generally of a very small size. What distinguished the capitalist from the simple commodity producing enterprises was the fact that the labourers in the capitalist enterprises could leave and therefore were sometimes able to bargain over their wages and conditions. This occurred despite the fact that these freedoms were supported by no legal rights, contractual or otherwise, and that the dominant ideology continued to deprecate them in the strongest possible terms. (For evidence of the existence of an urban, free labour market, see Wilkinson 1965, and for that of a rural one see Smith 1959.)

Many individual units of both kinds of enterprise were entirely dependent upon demands emanating from the feudal system, and so dependent upon the wider effects of its ideological thrall that they failed to survive its disappearance. Nevertheless, simple commodity and capitalist production as such were the principal economic beneficiaries of the collapse/destruction of feudalism. For the first time, their existence was entirely secure, if only negatively for the first four years after the Restoration given that the hitherto dominant feudal system no longer existed. These two modes of production, largely by default, defined the principal ways in which the production of 'traditional' commodities as well as that of newly introduced 'western' ones were to be carried out from then on (Nakamura 1983: 104 ff.). Of the two modes of production, simple commodity production was by far the most widespread, since it was, almost automatically, what was left in agriculture after the disappearance of Japan's 'feudalism without manors'. It was also usually all that was financially or technologically possible in manufacturing and services. Both forms of production sustained themselves in agriculture and expanded quite markedly in manufacturing. Small capitalist production grew at the expense of simple commodity production in both sectors, and *rentier* capitalism also grew at the expense of agriculture (Moore 1966: 275 ff.). However, neither simple commodity nor capitalist producers were among the direct beneficiaries of the larger-scale, state-sponsored investments in infrastructure and production, when these began to pay off towards the end of the period under review.

The newly established banks, which rapidly became the major providers of capital, preferred to invest in the even more newly established joint stock companies such as Mitsubishi or the few surviving and reconstructed large-scale merchant houses such as Mitsui. They were often related to the latter anyway through alliances of one kind or another. It was to such well-connected companies that the state preferred to sell its own enterprises, and at knock-down prices too. In this way several of the infamous *zaibatsu* (privately owned monopolistic combines) were created that were eventually to dominate the economy in the interwar period. Their presence, alongside that of the remarkably resilient small-scale production units, was to be one of the major reasons why the Japanese economy gained its particularly pronounced dualistic structure (Broadbridge 1966).

THE CREATION OF *TENNOSEI*

The extremely rapid construction of the basis for what was to become a very potent capitalist economy is what is best known today about the early Meiji era. What ought to be at least as widely known, but is not, is that this era also saw the equally rapid reconstruction of what might be called 'traditional patriarchalism' so that it became a much more diffuse but nevertheless extremely efficacious social ideology, centred on the *tenno* and reverence for his office.

Today, fortunately, it is far easier than it was to obtain knowledge of the construction and diffusion of this ideology, thanks largely to the work of Carol Gluck (1985). She has looked beyond the works of ideologues and read deeply into such other texts as 'village plans, teachers reports, statistical surveys, political speeches, diaries, memoirs, popular songs' (Gluck 1985: 14). Before summarising, reordering and slightly reworking some of Gluck's broader findings so that they fit better with the analytical framework lying behind the present study, it is important to emphasise, as she does, that, like the use of the term *tennosei* itself, the systematisation of the ideological reality to which the term refers occurred only at a later date: postwar in the case of the term and in the 1930s in that of the ideological reality. Nevertheless, as she also emphasises, this should not lead one either to doubt the ideology's earlier presence or to underestimate its earlier effects. The formation and effectivity of *tennosei* was continuous, if not uncontested (Bix 1986: pt 4; Irokawa 1985: chs 1–4), from the moment the Restoration movement commenced. Some of its roots were in the Shinto revivalism, nativism and scholarly political theory of the late Tokugawa period, as one would expect given the centrality of the *tenno* in the emergent anti-*bakufu* struggles (Earl 1964; Hall 1968a; Harootunian 1970). *Tennosei*'s supposedly non-ideological insistence on 'loyalty', 'filial piety' and duty more generally perfectly matched the non-party nature of the ongoing state-making politics and the practical significance of these values in a polity otherwise riven by a traditional and highly personalistic factionalism.

At first the ideological relationship sought by the *tenno* and his 'advisers' (*genro*) was a direct, representational one in the sense that the monarch was the head of the national family with little in the way of an intermediary concept of the nation to qualify the literalness of the claim so made. Appropriately, soon after the Restoration the Court embarked upon a series of six great journeys around the country to show itself in all its pomp. Also, Shintoism with its stress on ancestor worship, was made the established religion, if only for a few years. However, Gluck argues, such were the changes wrought within the society, such was its increasing and even then undeniable complexity, and so clearly were other, more narrowly economic institutions displacing the family as the core of social life, that it rapidly became apparent that the repetition of the homology of individual family/national family would no longer suffice as a plausible interpellative mechanism. Gradually, a recognition was forced on the *tenno* and the oligarchs that the ideological relationship they sought necessarily had to be an indirect rather than a direct one. The result was that the term *'tenno-*state' came to signify the concept 'nation' rather than refer directly to a real family of people.

However, this did not occur before strenuous efforts had been made to shape the ideological sphere so that what eventually came to be understood by the term 'nation' corresponded to the preferences of the rulers. Hence the content of the school curriculum (Passin 1965) and of the ideological training of the new conscript army (Norman 1940); hence also the obsessive tinkering with the institutional structure of the state and the incessant worrying over the various legal codes as well as over the Constitution, all then under construction, lest more than necessary should be given away; hence, finally, the practice of issuing pedagogic, Confucian-style Imperial Rescripts.

Tenno Meiji retreated from public life even before the promulgation of the Constitution in 1889 and increasingly spoke only in terms of nationalist generalities. However, despite all the ideological work just referred to, the aforementioned shift from a representational to a significatory interpellative strategy (not then understood in such terms, of course) meant that the ideological field was more open than it had been before. Discursive space became available for change by connotative intervention at the level of the concepts signified by critical terms; i.e. by offering divergent definitions of such critical signifiers as *tenno, Kokutai*, etc. In the event little advantage was taken of this space during the Meiji era. So limited were the opportunities available for the few who wished to voice alternative conceptions of what the nation should be, and so clearly foreign were most of their sources of inspiration, that even they, for the most part, had to couch their arguments in terms of *tennosei* concepts as well as words if they wished to have any chance of gaining a hearing (Irokawa 1985: chs 5–8).

In this way, then, the ideology became hegemonic whose principal signs and chains thereof were summarised most succinctly in the Imperial Rescript on Education that was issued in 1890, and which soon after every child knew by heart:

Know ye, our subjects!
Our Imperial ancestors have founded our empire on a
basis broad and everlasting and have deeply and firmly
implanted virtue; our subjects, ever united in loyalty and
filial piety, have from generation to generation illustrated
the beauty thereof.
This is the glory of the fundamental character of our
empire, and herein also lies the source of our education.
Ye, our subjects, be filial to your parents, affectionate to
your brothers and sisters; as husbands and wives be harmonious, as friends true; bear yourselves in modesty and
moderation; extend your benevolence to all; pursue learning and cultivate arts, and thereby develop your
intellectual faculties and perfect your moral powers; fur-
thermore, advance the public good and promote common
interests; always respect the constitution and observe the
laws; should any emergency arise, offer yourselves cou-
rageously to the state; and thus guard and maintain the
prosperity of our Imperial throne, coeval with heaven and
earth. So shall ye not only be our good and faithful subjects, but render illustrious the best traditions of our
forefathers.
The way here set forth is indeed the teaching bequeathed
by our Imperial ancestors, to be observed alike by their
descendants and subjects, infallible for all ages and true
in all places. It is our wish to lay it to heart in all reverence,
in common with you, our subjects, that we may all thus
attain to the same virtue.

LAW BEFORE THE *RECHTSSTAAT*

Because the early Meiji state was not a *Rechtsstaat*, the judiciary
had neither independence nor access to a unified and coherent
body of independently generated law that had to be universalistically applied to the citizenry (Henderson 1968b: 415 ff.). Nor,
despite the statutory granting of private property rights in 1872,
was it a straightforwardly capitalist legal system: capital's representatives possessed neither the need nor, even more certainly,
the means to restructure the law around the primacy of the
requirements of surplus labour appropriation.

In order to confirm these points and to give some substance

to the explanation for the absence of any threat by labour to capitalist possession in early Meiji Japan towards which they point, something must first be said about Tokugawa law since, with certain *ad hoc* alterations, it remained in force until the activation of the new and more explicitly capitalist Codes in the 1890s. What is more, and as is clear from Henderson's monumental work *Conciliation and Japanese Law* (1977), not only were many of the particulars of Tokugawa law repeated in the Codes, but also and significantly the general law/society relation continued to take basically the same form after their promulgation; i.e. one wherein, for example, property and family rights were established through state-administered registries (*koseki*) (Stevens and Takahashi 1975: 406 ff.) rather than courts, wherein the courts were anyway not as important as less formal conciliation fora, and where, finally and consequently, resort to the law was both difficult and socially deprecated.

Henderson has outlined the Tokugawa system in the following terms:

> The entirety of Tokugawa legal phenomena was a highly complex accumulation of imperial symbolism; a federalistic, doubledecked, feudal order; an elaborate status hierachy of great constitutional import resting solidly on the rice tax; a base of rural villages regulated intramurally by diverse customary laws covering the whole range of private transactions; and a Confucianistic family system – all made plausible by the isolation policy. As a whole these features may be regarded as a constitution in the English sense, articulated by some key, piecemeal, positive law decrees (e.g. the *buke-shohatto* and isolation decrees), customary practices, and precedents, all rationalised by orthodox Tokugawa Confucianistic philosophy (*shushigaku*). Clearly considerable positive law was generated by the shogunate (and *daimyo*), ... it is necessary first to understand the shogunate's own thinking about law itself. Essentially, it was a natural law approach (*ri* as formulated in *shushigaku*). The static legal order was regarded as both natural and just, and positive law decrees were largely declaratory of these laws of nature. Even in the positive law there was little concept of made-law, for the efficacy

of human endeavor to shape its environment was at the time low, and the concepts of law reflected that fact.

(Henderson 1968b: 393–4)

This very definitely feudalistic legal system pivoted around the maintenance of feudal landholding through the reinforcement of The Five Relationships (see the Rescript on Education, p.32) central to the neo-Confucianism that had become dominant if not hegemonic in the mid-seventeenth century. Nevertheless, as in Britain (Woodiwiss 1987b), it was made/able to find room for the existence of simple commodity and even capitalist production. This it did, despite or because of the existence of positive law to the contrary, through a device known as *dappo koi*. This was a legal fiction whereby it appeared that land had been transferred in payment of a debt rather than on payment of a price (Henderson 1974: 58–9). In this way a surrogate right of title to the means of production was established which is a necessary if not by itself a sufficient prerequisite for the possessory freedom necessary for any form of 'commodity production'. In the Japanese case the remaining ideological prerequisites for such freedom were met by traditional familial patriarchalism, which latterly was supported by the more diffuse patriarchalism of *tennosei*.

Most prominent among the discursive feudalistic particulars that were continued after the Restoration and indeed later repeated in the new Codes were those that related to the position of the *tenno* and to family relations (i.e. those most pertinent to the enforcement of patriarchalism and its component signs of 'loyalty' and 'filial piety'). The effects of these repetitions were not confined, however, to those areas to which they most directly referred, but gave a distinctive cast to legal discourse as a whole. Both the repetition of these particulars and of this result were linked through relations of mutual entailment to the continuation of the general form of the Tokugawa law/society relation in the post-Restoration social formation: where there is patriarchalist right and a means of successfully enforcing it, there is certainly no discursive space and perhaps little social need for other rights and/or other means of defining, deciding and enforcing disciplinary balances, and vice versa. Thus, in so far as there was little in the way of other rights, etc. to provide a counter to patriarchalism (for the persistence of conciliatory

34

fora, for example, see Henderson 1977: 209 ff.), there was also little to stop the latter reasserting itself. For a time it even seemed likely that ancient Chinese law would provide the model for Meiji jurists looking to the future (Chen 1981)!

As it happens another ancient but this time indigenous concept, *jori*, provided the means whereby traditional patriarchalism maintained itself as the Meiji era progressed and as it was absorbed by *tennosei*. This concept was extremely important during this period of rapid change because it referred to a source of law that could be invoked in the absence of positive or customary law. *Jori* is often translated as 'reason', but as Takayanagi (1976: 175 ff. ; see also Noda 1976: 222–4) has convincingly argued it is perhaps better translated as 'common sense'. Its discursive effects may be best illustrated by quoting from a treatise by a very prominent and liberalistically inclined Meiji lawyer, which shows how patriarchalism maintained itself even within the very discourse of property which otherwise might have been expected to have been its solvent:

> The issue of a law in 1872, which abolished the prohibition of sale of land and granted title deeds to landowners... and the establishment of joint-stock companies... mark[ed] the next step in the development of the separate property of house members. The court of law began to recognise house members' separate property in title-deeds... and the like, which they held in their own names, and afterwards in other things also, when their separate titles could be proved.
>
> In this manner individual property grew up *within the house*, that is to say, a house-member began to have his own property as an individual and not as a house-member. This change took place while the house-system was still in full vigour; and the consequence was that, the devolution of this new kind of property after the death of the owner resembled more the feudal escheat than succession. It *did not descend* to the children of the deceased, but *ascended to the house-head*.
>
> (Hozumi 1938: 172–3, empasis in the original)

Thus the presence of patriarchalist elements within legal discourse could prevent an owner, and one empowered as such by a positive law issuing from the *tenno* himself, from deciding upon the dispositions to be made of his property after his death. However, it takes little imagination to appreciate that the effects of the same presence on the freedom available to the employees of such a property owner were even more restrictive. Especially since in their regard, besides an edict of 1872 establishing freedom of contract, neither positive nor customary law contained any liberalistic counter signs, such as any right to freedom of association (Beer 1984: 46–53). Instead, Tokugawa prohibitions of peasant unions and collective bargaining were expressly continued (Marsland 1989: 29 ff. ; Nakamura 1962: 34).

CLASS STRUCTURE, INDUSTRIAL RELATIONS AND THE LAW

Having completed the outline of the principal structural features of early Meiji society, this text will turn now to providing a sketch of the class structure that was produced by them. It will then proceed to discuss further the bearing of the law's relatively autonomous development upon labour's position in the workplace.

On the basis of the data provided earlier and bearing in mind the overwhelming importance of simple commodity production, one may readily see that even in early Meiji Japan the conditions existed which allowed the existence of a set of specifically capitalist class positions. On the one hand, one may discern a set of positions produced by the coexistence of private possession of the means of production, patriarchal control over the production process and a legal right to title, even if the last was not totally secure. On the other hand, and by the same tokens, one may also discern a set of positions produced by exclusion from possession, subjection to patriarchal discipline and lack of any title. On the basis of the theoretical considerations outlined in the introduction, the existence of these two sets of positions at the levels of the social formation and the workplace means that their relations were defined by the appropriation of surplus-value and therefore that, in the absence of a non-petty bourgeois 'middle class', they represented rather clearly defined instances of a capitalist and a working class.

However, the particular character of the conditions of existence involved, especially the political and ideological ones, also

36

meant that in the workplace as well as in society more generally there was little space for conflict between the human subjects that embodied the two sets of positions. At neither level did the absolutist state provide many opportunities for such conflicts (i.e. there was no representative legislature and, of course, no encouragement of anything similar in the workplace). Nor did it allow the conflicts that did occur to continue for long (*vide* the fate, for example, of those who participated in the 'peasant' uprisings of the period, even when they were part of the otherwise largely bourgeois and professional Popular Rights Movement of the 1870s and 1880s, most famously the Chichibu rising of 1884, see Irokawa 1985: ch. 5).

Again, the incipient *tennosei* hegemony also tended to preempt any such conflicts at both levels with its insistence on loyalty, filial piety and duty. The effect of this chimed nicely with the authoritarian structures and still familialist nature of the discourses of production in the typical small factories, as well as with the predominance of female labour in the workforce in the larger enterprises such as the textile mills (Allinson 1975: 46, 51). The net effect of all this may be illustrated best by referring to the very vigorous efforts made by mill-owners to prevent any mobility on the part of their employees (Hane 1982: ch. 7; Taira 1970: 110 ff.). A partial exception to the almost totalitarian constraint on the freedoms of labourers may be found in the conditions obtaining in some of the larger enterprises, such as the shipyards and ironworks (Gordon 1985: ch. 1). Here the majority of unskilled workers were subject to the patriarchal discipline imposed by the labour sub-contractors (*oyakata*) who hired them and thus their relations tended to replicate the highly repressive *oyabun/kobun* relationships of the feudal period (for the extremely oppressive conditions in Mitsui's Takashima mines, see Taira 1970: 106). However, the small number of skilled workers, whether certificated or self-taught, often enjoyed considerable freedom to come and go as they pleased and bargain, albeit individualistically, over wages and conditions.

CONCLUSION

To conclude, neither social conflict in general nor industrial conflict in particular attained the intensity necessary for the actions of the subjects involved to have any significant disintegrative effects on the structures that positioned them. Adequate legal and customary means were available to facilitate and, if necessary, enforce transfers of ownership and other exchanges, including those that occurred in the labour market (cf. the United States in the first half of the nineteenth century, Woodiwiss 1987b). But because of the socially pervasive presence of patriarchy and a highly retributive criminal law there was little social need for, as well as little discursive possibility of, any special body of labour law, whether of the individual or the collective variety. This said, mention should be made, nevertheless, of a draft factory bill produced by the state Industrial Bureau in 1883, which interestingly was largely concerned with discipline and mobility problems (Garon 1987: 20). However, the authors of the bill had to wait a long time before the import of their labours was recognised. Outside of their circle, apart from some regret on the part of employers that contracts of employment appeared to be unenforceable, little cause for the existence of labour law could be found in the conditions facing the small, capitalist sector, and none whatsoever in those facing the large, simple commodity one. In the capitalist sector, capital felt little threat to either its powers of possession and control or to the legitimacy of its title to any profits that might be produced, and labour was not in a position to voice let alone to follow through on any such threat. In the simple commodity sector, of course, no bifurcation of classes occurred anyway, disciplinary and ideological relations really were patriarchal, and therefore the fit was good between the workplace and national levels of social relations and the mutual reinforcement between them was highly effective.

The proximate cause, then, of the absence of labour law from early Meiji Japan is the same as that for the extreme autonomies of the political and legal systems from capitalist economic relations, and it may be found in the dominance within the economy of petty commodity production and the reciprocally reinforcing relations between it and the extant patriarchal political and ideological relations of the wider society.

Now, for the first time, the three questions that structure this narrative may be answered. The question as to why and under what circumstances the law took an interest in industrial relations in this period may be summarily answered as follows: the law entered industrial relations settings as a consequence of the changes initiated by the Meiji Restoration, as, relatedly, the nature of the dominant mode of production changed from simple commodity production to capitalism, and as, therefore, the reciprocity of national and workplace social relations was disrupted. The question as to how and on what basis whatever legal interventions that occurred were decided may be answered as follows: as had traditionally been the case, the law only entered the workplace where there were allegations of criminal wrong-doing, most often involving violence and theft, or where there were fears of more widespread civil commotion; thus the outcomes of any cases were determined by the criminal law and by whatever pressure employers and/or state servants brought to bear on the judiciary. Finally, the question as to the disciplinary consequences of this legal regime may be answered as follows: despite their many local and short-term successes, the effects of the outcomes of such cases were ultimately insufficient to prevent the emergence of a labour movement determined to challenge some aspects of the existing structures of industrial relations (Marsland 1989). However, neither the emergence of this movement nor any of the myriad other social changes that occurred later were sufficient to produce a radical transformation of either labour's legal status or the class-structural and social context which fixed it as an inferior status. The law applicable to labour remained the criminal law and, therefore, in Kahn-Freund's terms, 'repressive'.

NOTES

1 The phrase 'properly capitalist states' refers to states where the exercise of overall social discipline is premissed upon the protection of the rights of capitalist private property owners and upon, therefore, the presence of capitalist law as *the* discourse of empowerment. This said, like absolutist states, which typically exercised overall social discipline on the basis of feudal law and yet allowed the development of capitalist relations of production (Woodiwiss 1987b: 456–8), capitalist states may nevertheless exert their disciplinary powers in the pursuit of goals legitimated by discourses other than those that fundamentally empower them. The only requirements are that such discourses should be legally articulated and, more importantly, that they should not be subverted by other coexisting legal or other discourses. Thus both kinds of state may be said to be possessed of a certain inherent capacity for 'relative autonomy', the occurrence and degree of which will vary with the social–structural

context and the balances of forces obtaining in particular social formations.
2 In this limited regard at least the Koza faction's insistence on the antipathy between absolutism and capitalism is salutary.
3 The next three sections of this chapter are revised versions of parts of Woodiwiss 1990c.

2

CONSTITUTIONAL JAPAN AND THE IMPOSSIBILITY OF LABOUR LAW

By the 1890s, the economic dominance of simple commodity production was being strongly challenged in value terms by capitalism; a fact formally recognised by the promulgation of the Civil Code and its strengthening of the rights of private property and broadening of the freedoms of contracting parties. However, as indicated earlier, this recognition was accompanied by the mutually reinforcing, combined repetition of many feudal doctrinal particulars and by the persistence of the traditional law/society relationship. The result of this was that the law also aided the reproduction of other sets and modes of relations apart from those normally, if ethnocentrically, considered to be appropriate to capitalism. Legally, the incoherence that this bespoke replicated that of the early Meiji period. Given the arrival of a *Rechtsstaat*, however, the problems that resulted were laid more often at the doors of jurists, whose powers of interpretation they tested most severely – to breaking point in some cases during the 1930s. Further, the jurists' discomfort was intensified and made all but inescapable by the slightness of the qualifications to the state's absolutism brought about by the passage of the Meiji Constitution, and by the ongoing elaboration of *tennosei* ideology. In what follows it will be argued that it was this coexistence of the old and the new that gave to the Japanese social formation and its new *Rechtsstaat* their particular characters and so rendered impossible the appearance of a system of labour law properly so-called in either the Taisho or early Showa periods.

THE NEW *TENNO*-STATE

Given the complexity of the forces underlying the Restoration process, it is not surprising that some objections were raised against the unalloyed absolutism of the early Meiji period. These were particularly strong with respect to the failure to maintain the Charter Oath's commitment to the establishment of a representational component to the state and the repression of those who complained about it. Eventually, in 1881, the dissidents, who came from diverse but largely rural, capitalist backgrounds, formed the Jiyuto Party. A year later, those who came from similarly diverse but largely urban, capitalist backgrounds formed the Kaishinto Party. Interestingly and perhaps because capitalism had a longer history in the countryside than the towns, the former was somewhat more liberalistic than the latter in that it framed its demands more often in the language of individual or popular rights. Both parties were tiny and their demand for representation did not apply to, was seldom heard by and anyway was seldom understood amongst, the wider population. Nevertheless, it was quickly met. This was largely thanks to the not entirely fortuitous coincidence between the parties' foundings and the occurrence of a serious riot in Tokyo in connection with a major scandal over a planned sale of state-owned resources in Hokkaido to private capital at a considerable discount. This had been brought to the public's attention by finance minister Okuma, who then resigned, founded Kaishinto and petitioned the *tenno* for the opening of a legislative assembly in 1883. The *tenno* accepted the petition but postponed the date of implementation to 1890.

In the meantime, the continued existence of the two parties was made very difficult (they dissolved themselves in 1883 and 1884), representatives were dispatched to Europe to examine various sets of constitutional arrangements, and measures were taken to prepare the institutional ground for the ready reception of whatever specific arrangements were eventually to be preferred by the oligarchy. Although it was to be some time before the detailed specification of the arrangements was completed, their general outline must have been known from the beginning in order for appropriate preparatory measures to have been undertaken. Like the reorganisation of central/local relations carried out in the latter half of the 1870s in connection with the initial form of the *tenno*-state, the preparatory measures prefigured the centralisation and sustained executive-centredness of the new structure very accurately. Thus, in 1885, the nobility was re-invented in order that a future upper house might be staffed, and a cabinet was set up that was separate from but answerable to the *tenno* and to the exclusion of any future legislature. As McLaren (1965: 148) long ago recognised, when a representative legislature was at last established, it was '*fitted into* the bureaucratic structure of the central government and *subordinated*... strictly to the oligarchy...' (emphasis added). In other words, the formulation of the Constitution provides a graphic illustration of the thoroughly utilitarian rather than what is commonly supposed to be the imitative nature of much Japanese 'western learning'; i.e. in this case the Prussian Constitution was not so much a source of inspiration as a useful guide in the resolution of certain technical problems encountered in the pursuit of preset goals.

This was made very clear when co-draftsman Roesler's objections were blithely dismissed and the Constitution was left to begin in the following personalistic and far from Prussian, let alone *zweckrationale*, manner:

The Empire of Japan shall be reigned over and governed by a line of Emperors unbroken for ages eternal.

The ordinance power thus rested in the hands of a *tenno*, whose prerogative, outside of the extensive areas entirely reserved to it (i.e. military, police, public welfare, constitutional revision and emergency powers), was constrained only by the need to request retroactive *Diet* approval for any uses of the power that had not been so approved beforehand. Even the necessity of the *Diet*'s approval of the budget represented little by way of a constraint on executive power, since the previous year's appropriation would stand again should the *Diet* not approve a particular budget. The *Diet* itself consisted of two houses: an upper house of peers elected by and from the nobility and supplemented by imperial appointees and members of the *tenno*'s family; and a lower house of representatives elected by the population at large according to a property-based franchise provided for in a separate piece of legislation, which had the effect of limiting the franchise to only a little over 1 per cent of the population. (The

Constitution also provided for a judiciary and specified certain rights and duties due to and from subjects, which are more appropriately discussed below.)

Notwithstanding the continuing power of the *genro* (Hackett 1968), the increasing coherence of the bureaucracy, the growing confidence of the military, the extremely restricted nature of the *Diet*'s powers, the venality of politicians, occasional assassinations, and the consequent instability of cabinets, the latter became, in 1919, the creatures of whatever might be the majority party for some thirteen years thereafter (Scalapino 1968). This time, in a striking demonstration of the importance of legal and structural possibilities in the shaping of polities, the now legal parties succeeded in gaining a certain institutional and ideological weight despite the oligarchy's strong disapproval. The two most important parties to emerge after 1918 were the Seiyukai and the Minseito. The former represented a longstanding (since 1900) merger of the rural forces that had supported Jiyuto with certain sections of the bureaucracy. And the latter, which this time was the slightly more liberalistic of the two, represented a development of a later (1915) fusion of the urban forces that had supported Kaishinto with certain other bureaucratic elements (Garon 1987: 47–9, 50, 144, 138–9; Scalapino 1968).

Despite all that they owed to legally created structural opportunities, nothing the party governments did strengthened the position of the legislature, with the possible exception of the broadening of the franchise to all males of more than twenty-five years of age in 1925. This was a failure that was to have serious consequences, given that the military (Halliday 1976: chs 4, 5) and the bureaucracy (Silberman 1982) were gaining both expertise and wider social prestige on their own behalves, and in a world that was about to be subjected to geo-political and economic stresses that would severely test all representative institutions.

The elections of the 1930s saw the *Diet* majority alternating between the two major parties and the gradual growth of extreme nationalist and moderate socialist or farmer–labour parties. In the 1937 election the two socialist parties gained 12 per cent of the house seats (on their development see Scalapino 1953; 1983). However, because of the victory over Russia in 1905, the annexation of Korea in 1910, and the successful, if unauthorised, takeover of Manchuria in 1932, which saw a sharp intensification of the ongoing encroachment on China, the armed forces gradually enhanced their political–economic and ideological clout within the state and society. They, more than any other institution, short of the imperial office itself, embodied *tennosei*. Because of this and the growing importance of military spending as a proportion of state expenditure, they came into conflict with civilian politicians and, latterly, gained power over them.

The bureaucracy, for its part, successfully fashioned and operated a linkage mechanism between the state and civil society, which Silberman (1982: 243 ff.) has termed 'limited pluralism'. This maintained the primacy of the state over society and of the executive over the rest of the state. It thus provided an institutional context within which the anyway substantial means of disciplinary intervention represented by the police might be deployed in the service of *tennosei*. This mechanism appears to have been very effective in containing any potentially disruptive groupings which emerged and it gained institutional form in the first decades of the twentieth century. Whether they were organisations of army reservists, businessmen, youths or, eventually, trade unionists, none of these groups achieved sufficient autonomy from the state to be capable of articulating their demands on their own terms. As a result of making use of the state's virtual monopoly of the legal expertise which Tokyo University had been set up to provide, such groups were provided with legal identities on certain rather rigorous conditions, some opportunities to express their views, and access to conciliatory bodies when they had grievances.

In Silberman's view:

By at least 1931 the high-water mark of limited pluralism as a structure of authority had been reached and this pluralism was already being transformed. The transformation was taking place by the very success of the bureaucracy in delimiting the boundaries of legitimate interests. Already by the mid-twenties the rural sectors of interest, despite discontent over issues of tenancy and the import of colonial agricultural products, had been sufficiently atomised and coopted so as no longer to pose a serious problem in terms of class based interest. By the early thirties labor and small-scale, marginal enterprises had been conflated into the structure of large-scale economic organizations, where they were reduced to passivity and subject to control.

(Silberman 1982: 247)

In this way, then, most of the potentially critical groups were absorbed within the state and a penumbra of state-sponsored organisations. Thus an effective mechanism of rule was available should the legislature and its parties cease to be favoured by the powerholders, or in more formal terms should the *tenno* be convinced of their superfluity. This, of course, is what actually happened in 1932. The army refused to supply a minister of war to any cabinet headed by a party leader. Thereafter, despite some initial resistance from the parties, some industrialists and the labour movement, and despite some internal conflicts, the armed forces ruled through the cabinet, willingly assisted by a 'renovationist' bureaucracy, and with little attention to the legislature. This state of affairs was formalised by the passage of the *National General Mobilisation Act* in 1938. The parties were dissolved in October 1940 and the hitherto internalised and absorptive method of rule was made explicit by the formation of The Imperial Rule Assistance Association in the same year. This said, it is important to note that, despite efforts in this direction (Hirschmeier and Yui 1981: 247 ff.), capital was not nationalised, nor did the state take on a fascist form (Halliday 1976: 133 ff.). The ease with which a return to an absolutism could be attained made both moves unnecessary.

THE EMERGENCE OF A DUAL ECONOMY

From the 1890s onwards and largely under its own gathering momentum, the economy grew steadily and latterly rather rapidly until the end of the second decade of the twentieth century. The speed-up may be explained by reference to: (1) the renewed state interest and investment in the economy during the mid–1890s in connection with the adoption of a more aggressive foreign policy; (2) the associated establishment of heavy metallurgical industries such as iron, steel and shipbuilding; (3) the regained power to impose protective tariffs thanks to the revision in 1911 of the 'unequal treaties' of the early nineteenth century; and (4) the creation of market opportunities by colonial expansion and the onset of the First World War. Progress slowed markedly in the 1920s as these stimuli lost their potency. It only recommenced in the 1930s as again, and for the same reasons, the state's interest in the economy revived. This time the interest centred on agriculture, the chemical and electrical engineering industries and, of course, the armaments industry (for the general trajectory, see Nakamura 1983; and for developments in specific industries, see Allen 1946).

Within the general trajectory just outlined some rather dramatic structural changes occurred. Agriculture lost ground to industry. Its contribution to the GDP fell from 45.2 per cent in 1885 to 17.6 per cent in 1935 (Nakamura 1983: 22). 'Traditional' (i.e. simple commodity and small capitalist) industry lost ground to 'modern' (i.e. medium and large-scale) capitalist industry. Its contribution to manufacturing output in value terms fell from 97.1 per cent in 1884 to 25.8 per cent in 1930 (Hirschmeier and Yui 1981: 153–9; Nakamura 1983: 80). However, as late as 1935 44.3 per cent of the labour force were still employed in the largely 'traditional' tertiary sector and fully 87.9 per cent of the non-tertiary labour force were still employed in 'traditional' enterprises, evenly split between agricultural and industrial ones. In sum, by the same year only 12.1 per cent of the non-tertiary labour force were employed in 'modern' enterprises (Nakamura 1983: 28). The very striking survival, in comparative terms, of 'traditional' enterprises as very important employers requires some explanation. Not only is it germane to the present concern with the reasons for the continuation of the early Meiji legal stance as regards trade unions despite the establishment of a *Rechtsstaat*, but also to the understanding of the nature of Japan's present day dual economy.

Following Nakamura's analysis (1983: 81, 83 ff. 191, 218 ff., 227 ff.) in the main, the chief reasons for the survival of 'traditional' modes of production in the industrial sphere during the prewar period were threefold. First, depending as they did on state priorities and state or bank finance rather than self-generated funds, 'modern' enterprises became established only in a small number of markets and therefore offered little direct competition to the smaller enterprises, especially with regard to consumer goods. Second, apart from the period of particularly rapid growth on the part of 'modern' enterprises which was associated with the First World War, such enterprises also offered little direct competition to the 'traditional' enterprises in the labour market. Moreover, during the 1920s, the 'modern' enterprises engaged in a series of rigorous 'rationalisation' or labour-shedding exercises as they sought to cut costs in the face of unfavourable market conditions. Third, the wage differential favouring workers in 'modern' companies that gradually emerged contributed to the difficulties already faced by the incipient unions because of unemployment and the state's developing anti-union strategy. Taking these points together, concentration increased in the markets in which the 'modern' enterprises competed as some of them failed to adjust, i.e. some of the large enterprises got even larger. Meanwhile the 'traditional' enterprises benefited from the general rise in the price level that accompanied economic development because, in the absence of cross-sectoral unions, they did not have to compete with the larger ones on wages, i.e. the small enterprises survived.

THE RULE OF *TENNOSEI*

A large part of the story of how *tennosei* ceased to be merely like 'the east wind in a horse's ear' (Gluck 1985: 14) and became instead 'a weight over the eyes' (Irokawa 1985: 9) has already been outlined in the preceding sections of this chapter. It is the story of how imperial patriarchy was formally established as the ruling ideology with the promulgation of the Constitution, and of how it was broadcast by Imperial Rescripts and school textbooks, etc. (Irokawa 1985: 299 ff.). What remains to be described is the relationship between these developments and *tennosei*'s application in economic settings so as to ameliorate the social tensions created in the wake of capitalism's progress; in the wake, therefore, of the disruption (interestingly referred to as 'domicide' by Irokawa 1985: 288) of the original, familial patriarchy of the farms and workshops. This process, and the ambivalence towards capitalism that it displays, will be discussed further below. But first, attention must be paid to the general development of *tennosei* during the prewar period.

Even after the promulgation of the Constitution and the activation of the Codes, the qualifications to absolutism and the linked encroachments of capital in the state sphere were very limited. Nevertheless, they were sufficient to undermine the plausibility of the more literal readings of *tennosei*'s patriarchalism and so to allow the voicing of alternatives, namely liberalism and socialism. However, neither alternative was articulated, by their more influential proponents at least, in a way that was free of *tennosei* elements. And neither, therefore, presented much resistance when the proponents of the one deployed their *tennosei* inflected discourse against the other. In other words, each ideology claimed the paternity of the *Kokutai* and in reproducing itself reproduced *tennosei* also. Capital, for example, opted for 'patriarchy' or 'our beautiful customs' over 'the right to manage' as the sign that it preferred to see governing the discourses of production and so legitimating the managerial prerogative. In so doing it weakened its own ability to withstand *tennosei* in other spheres and with regard to other policy areas, crucially as regards the nature of the polity itself and agricultural policy.

Similarly, labour, even organised labour, deployed patriarchal rhetoric in voicing their criticisms and demands (Crump 1983, *passim*). A good example is provided by the petition discovered by Marsland (1989: 135) and drawn-up by a socialist-led metalworkers organisation in 1900 as part of its campaign *against* the patriarchal, *oyakata*-type managerial structure of The Japan Railway Company:

> All the Company's workers, including we humble workers, do sincerely feel that deep gratitude for the many life-sustaining benefits the company has bestowed upon its workers must be expressed. However, pressed by circumstances, we open our hearts on the following points, and wonder if we might not wish for them:
> That all workers be treated fairly and impartially.
> That a training school for young workers be set up.
> That the occupational names be reformed.
> That better treatment be given to the workers.
> That hourly pay be reformed to daily pay.
> That public holidays be observed at the workshops.
> That company housing be given to the workers, except that this be limited to those that live in the country (rather than the cities).
> We humbly point out that it would be most fortunate if the Company would, on the basis of its consideration of the situation, judge the above points, and if it accepts them, implement them with haste.
> With thanks and a hundred bows.

Entrapped as labour appeared to remain within such a discourse, it is hardly surprising that, when subject to even greater ideological pressure than that bespoken by this petition, they too were ultimately unable to resist opting for 'patriarchy' over 'collective bargaining' as the sign that they too preferred to see governing the discourses of production. Thus it was because *tennosei* was latterly able to present itself, unchallenged by either capital or labour, as the protector of the whole society (i.e. not just of the rich and the patriarchs), that the apparently voluntary *tenko* (conversion) of so many socialists was possible during the 1930s (Marshall 1967: ch. 5). *Tennosei*'s hegemonic position meant that the alternative discourses incorporated its signifiers as their own and sought only to change what they signified by articulating them with their own particular signs. In this way they attempted to exclude one another, but in the event they merely negated one another.

Of course, it was not solely *tennosei*'s hegemonic status that accounted for its triumph, but also the unfavourableness of the political and especially economic conditions to the alternatives. To recapitulate, in the early years of the reign of *Tenno* Taisho (1912–26) the economy grew quickly. Although much of the prosperity was a product of successful military (i.e. state) ventures, capital nevertheless gained a greater measure of political power than before (this was the era when party cabinets became established). In addition, civil society more generally gained a greater measure of autonomy from the state than before (this was the era when a socialist party became established). It even seemed that *tennosei* itself was losing its grip (Harootunian 1974). It seems reasonable to suppose that had the economy remained healthy all these developments would have continued.

In the event the economy did not remain healthy. Economic development was slow for much of the interwar period, and the 'modern', capitalist sector remained small. Nevertheless, the changes in social relationships in cities, villages, workplaces, on farms and even in families were sufficiently marked that the term 'patriarchal' seldom represented a totally accurate description of them any more, let alone represented an unchallengeable source of ethical imperatives. The disjunction between *tennosei* and discursive reality became even more marked as the economy revived again in the 1930s. But by this time the military had displaced the parties as the body that decided on the composition of the cabinet. The ironic result was thus that precisely as *tennosei*, thanks to the military, became unchallengeable at the national level, the disintegration of its conditions of existence accelerated because of the economic effects of militarisation. Hence, perhaps, the need to enunciate it formally and for the first time as a totality in the *Kokutai no Hongi* prepared under the direction of the Ministry of Education and published in 1937. Hence also, perhaps, the straining to convince, noted by Gluck (1985: 282), apparent in the baroque opening passage of the same text, which contrasts so strongly with the matter-of-factly theocratic discourse of the preamble to the Constitution (see p.43 and Nakano 1923: 259) and the simple certainty of the Rescript on Education, both of which address similar themes:

> The unbroken line of Emperors, receiving the Oracle of the Founder of the Nation, reign eternally over the Japanese Empire. This is our eternal and immutable *kokutai*. Thus, founded on this great principle, all the people, united as one great family-nation in heart and obeying the Imperial Will, enhance indeed the beautiful views of loyalty and filial piety. This the glory of our *kokutai*. This *kokutai* is the eternal and unchanging basis of our nation and shines resplendent throughout our history. Moreover, its solidarity is proportionate to the growth of the nation and is, together with heaven and earth, without end. We must, to begin with know with what active brilliance this fountainhead shines within the reality of the founding of our nation.
>
> (quoted by Gluck 1985: 283)

LAW UNDER THE *RECHTSSTAAT*

Despite constitutional provision for an independent judiciary and guarantees of a long list of personal freedoms, the invented term *Staatrechts* might be more descriptive of the legal realities in prewar Japan than *Rechtsstaat*. One reason why is suggested by the unintended humour present in the rather strained effort by Baron Ito, a member of the *genro* and chair of the drafting committee, to find a democratic significance in the use of the traditional phrase 'the great treasure' to describe the people. This culminates in the following quotation from a speech by an assistant chief of police on the occasion of a pardon: 'You must henceforth become the great treasure of the land, and must make ready to pay your taxes' (Ito 1889: 35). More seriously, the legal primacy of the state's executive interest is apparent in such constitutional provisions as: the divinity of the sovereign; the uniquely extensive ordinance powers reserved to the *tenno* (Nakano 1923: 3, 6, 13, 18); and in the very restricted powers granted to the *Diet*. It is also apparent in: the limitations on the judiciary's powers in relation to the activities of the state; the absence of sanctions that the judiciary may exercise on its own behalf, such as the power to fine or jail for contempt (Haley 1982a); and the qualified nature of most of the rights granted to the citizenry. The limitations on the judiciary's powers *vis-à-vis* the remainder of the state are clear from Article 61, which provides as follows:

> No suit at law, which relates to rights alleged to have been infringed by the illegal measures of the administrative authorities, and which shall come within the competency of the Court of Administrative Litigation specially established by law, shall be taken cognizance of by a Court of Law.

In his simultaneously published commentary Ito explained part of the somewhat cynical reasoning behind this limitation in the following terms: 'administrative expediency is just what judicial authorities are not ordinarily apt to be conversant with' (Ito 1889: 110).

In what Beckmann (1957: 94) has aptly referred to as 'another repository of authoritarianism', the Constitution's 'bill of rights', only two of the rights are specified in an unqualified manner, that of freedom of abode and movement, and that of arrest and trial according to law. Each of the others, whether rights of privacy, property, religious belief, speech and association (i.e. those most central to a democratic public sphere and the entrenchment of themselves as well as of other citizenship rights) is qualified in their very promulgation by reference to the possibility of some limitations being imposed upon them by the passage of some later law. Again it is instructive to note the rationale given by Ito:

> as every one of these double-edged tools can easily be misused, it is necessary for the maintenance of public order, to punish by law and *prevent by police measures* delegated by law any disturbance... of the peace of the country... (emphasis added).
>
> (Ito 1889: 55–6)

The italicised phrase proved to be of particular pertinence for labour, as will be explained below. Anticipating this explanation somewhat, Uyehara's reflection on some twenty years of experience of life under the Constitution, may usefully be inserted here:

> There is nothing in the constitution to safeguard the rights and liberties of the people from the permanent executive officials.
>
> (Uyehara 1910: 132)

In sum, despite the plaudits of United States Supreme Court Justice, Oliver Wendell Holmes, which in retrospect are harder to understand than those of Herbert Spencer, Japan remained a 'theocratic–patriarchal' state (Hozumi 1938: 86) even after the passage of the Constitution. Nor, unsurprisingly, need the accuracy of this judgement be significantly challenged when one takes into account the various legal Codes that came into force in the following decade. This said, it might just have been otherwise in the area of private law, if the original, French-inspired Civil Code had come into force. The various books of this latter Code did in fact become law in the course of the year 1890, but a vigorous campaign was waged against it and, for rather different if equally mixed reasons, the accompanying Commercial Code. First, the Codes' date of enforcement was postponed and then they were rewritten. The reasons for the campaign are made clear in the following paraphrase of an article by Hozumi Yatsuka (the very conservative brother of the more liberal jurist referred to earlier):

he vehemently took exception to the individualistic tone

of the Civil Code... he emphasised the fact that the transplanting of the Civil Code based on the principle of individualistic Christianity in this land founded on ancestor worship... not only ran counter to our time-honoured morals and manners, but also to the great principle of education and culture... revealed in the Imperial Rescript on Education.

(Nakamura 1962: 86, n. 15)

In the area of central concern here, the problem was, as Mukai and Toshitani (1967: 46) have put it, how to square the need for freedom in the relations between enterprises with the equally imperative need to respect the patriarchal authority structure (i.e. the 'gentle ways and beautiful customs') within enterprises. On Nakamura's analysis (1962: 90–2; see also Hozumi 1938: 173, ff.), such a campaign was unnecessary. The original Code gave ample support to the status aspects of patriarchy, for example as they affected the honorific position of the head of the 'house'. The Civil Code was rewritten nevertheless and came into force in 1898. It strengthened patriarchal authority relative to the House. In addition, although it reclassified leases as obligations rather than real rights and abolished certain customary, feudal rights in land (*usufruct*, use, domicile), it also allowed the validity of others (e.g. *emphyteusis*, a grant of land for ever, or a long period upon condition that an annual rent is paid) – the latter for fifty years after the promulgation of the Code, regardless of whether or not the land was owned by another (Ishii 1968: 577, ff.; Nakamura 1962: 98–100).

To most modern readers (e.g. Haley 1982b) the conservatism of the revised Code has been seen to lie in the limited nature of the restraints on capital that it contained, whereas from the present perspective it lay in the continued existence of any such restraints. Because of these restraints, although the Code contained a thoroughly modern definition of ownership (i.e. one that expressly protected the capitalist right to profit from the ownership of property), it cannot be said that the freedom of capital was *the* premiss upon which the Code operated and therefore that it articulated a discourse different from and opposed to theocratic–patriarchalism. Read, as it had to be, in conjunction with the Constitution and, as it usually was, in the light of *tennosei* commentaries on the latter such as Ito's (Pittau 1967: 199), the Code did little to enhance capital's freedom:

> the right of property is under the powers of the state. It ought therefore to be subordinated to the latter....

> When it is necessitated by public benefit private individuals may be compelled *nolens volens* to part with their property....

> (Ito 1889: 50)

It failed therefore to establish a substantial discursive counterweight to *tennosei* or the *tenno*-state'–not surprisingly, given that many capitalist *Diet* members, and not just farmers, were as vocal in their support for the postponement and rewriting of the Codes as the nobility. Nevertheless, in line with and even in advance of the economic, political and more general ideological developments associated with the period of 'Taisho Democracy', the law also but all too briefly saw a retreat of 'theocratic–patriarchalism'.

Building on earlier reforms, the promulgation of the Constitution and the Codes gave a measure of independence to the judiciary, even though the courts were understood to exercise juridical power only 'in the name of the emperor'. The judiciary quickly established a degree of independence in fact when, in 1891, it resisted government pressure for a more severe penalty than the law allowed in connection with an attempt on the life of the visiting Russian crown prince (Henderson 1968b: 424–6). Despite an understandable early pedagogical concern with exegetal discussions of the Codes (for the classic English language example, see De Becker's *Annotated Civil Code of Japan*, 1909), and despite a preference for very formalistic, 'black letter' techniques of interpretation, jurists and the judiciary gradually became more interpretatively active. They expanded and qualified the role allowed them by the Constitution's continued, if more narrowly circumscribed, allowance of '*jori*' as a source of law (Henderson and Haley 1978: 375). And they successfully claimed a place for the judiciary's precedents as an additional source of law (Itoh 1970: 779–85). This permitted certain jurists to take advantage of the significatory space within *tennosei* mentioned earlier (see p.31) and to attempt to qualify its power somewhat.

The most dramatic result of the freedom that jurists gained in this way was Minobe's, for a time, widely accepted critique ('the organ theory') of the literal *'tennosei'* interpretation of the Constitution (Miller 1965). According to this critique, the office of *tenno* embodied the sovereign power of the state as a whole in its executive, legislative and judicial forms and hence was neither superior to its component institutions, nor beyond their purview. On this basis Minobe argued that the *tenno*, even when exercising what might otherwise seem to be his reserved ordinance powers, not only could not impose his will on the component institutions but also was himself subject to legislative and judicial constraint. However, as Banno (1987: 9–10) has recently made clear, significantly, even Minobe had some difficulty reconciling his theory with the unambiguous nature of the *tenno*'s position of military leadership. Nevertheless, throughout the Taisho period and into the 1930s this theory held sway amongst jurists. Then, like Minobe himself, it fell victim to the rising tide of *tennosei*. In this case *tennosei*'s embodiment was one Professor Uesugi, who revived the absolutist and literalist theory that had been enunciated first by Minobe's late and very conservative Tokyo University colleague Hozumi Yatsuka. As Uesugi said, when looking back over his life:

> I felt deeply that our *kokutai* was unique among the nations. I realized that in Japan, whose national foundations were without equal in the world and whose historical development was also completely different, the essence of the constitution ... by its very nature had to be different from theirs. And I came to harbour the unshakable conviction that a clear consciousness of the imperial *kokutai* and a firm belief in reverence for the emperor must be the foundation and essence of the study of the Japanese constitution.
>
> (Minear 1970: 190)

Given that judges no less than other citizens, and perhaps more so since they were acting 'in the name of the emperor', were subject to interpellation by *tennosei*, the autonomy they claimed for themselves eventually failed to protect the citizenry and any of the latter's rights against repressive acts undertaken by the state. (For the parallel history of the rise and fall of an 'abuse of rights' (tort) doctrine favouring less powerful parties, see Henderson and Haley 1978.) As the amended Peace Preservation Law of 1941 stated, 'anyone who appears like they *might want* to change the absolutism of the emperor (was to be arrested)'(emphasis in the original 1970, quoted in Beer 1984: 66; see also Mitchell 1976: 201–5).

Thus the arrival of a *Rechtsstaat* ultimately failed to secure a more open public sphere let alone a freer private one. The public sphere remained too closed thanks to the limitations on the liberal–democratic freedoms, whilst the private sphere remained too open thanks to the aid given to state surveillance by the continuing free access to the various registries and their highly personal information (Henderson and Haley 1978: 411). Both failures were accelerated by renewed state encouragement of conciliation (*chotei*) as an alternative to legal proceedings in the 1920s and 1930s (Haley 1978: 373–8). This began with the passage of the Land-Lease and House Lease Conciliation Law of 1922 and culminated with that of the Special Wartime Civil Affairs Law of 1942. This development continued and encouraged the restraints on capital in relation to the sale and use of land that the rewriting of the Constitution had achieved, adding to them substantial restrictions on the rights of creditors (Haley 1982b: 138; Henderson 1974: 212–14), although presumably only in cases where the debtors were those, like farmers, of whom the state approved.

In sum, whether one prefers the term *Rechtsstaat* or *Staatrechts*, the *rechts* involved were clearly neither capitalist in any simple way, nor by the same token capable of offering much resistance to *tennosei*. Thus, insofar as the Constitution protected the freedom of the *tenno*-state to act as it pleased, and insofar as the new Codes repeated this protection, they perpetuated the presence of 'patriarchy' within legal discourse. 'Skilfully interwoven' (Mukai and Toshitani 1967: 46) though patriarchy and capitalist right most definitely were in the two texts, this did not prevent the discourse they made possible becoming incoherent and, latterly, dominated by *tennosei*. The content of the texts did not permit that overall commitment to the value of 'consistency' within a system of legal discourse which is a prerequisite of legal autonomy and therefore of 'the rule of law' (see p.12). For this reason, the Codes failed to provide much discursive resistance to the resurgence of *tennosei* in the 1930s, although as the authors of *Kokutai no Hongi* regretfully admitted, this does not mean that 'our people have always been free of harbouring ideas of profit'. In the same movement, a strong body of administrative law that could protect the citizenry from the state also failed to emerge (Haley 1986; Henderson 1968b: 426 ff. ; Wada 1977). Thus the attractiveness of conciliation to those with private grievances was maintained – why risk everything in a court where, if the grievance was against the actions of someone in authority, the odds were stacked in the latter's favour, and when it could be settled, even if not judged, in another way or another forum, especially one that emphasised some of the obligations incurred by patriarchs?

The acceptance which the latter question invites was one that, like many other groups, organised, let alone unorganised, labour eventually found very hard to resist: this was not just because it was subject to capitalist as well as state patriarchy in the courts and the workplace. Positive acts of legal and police repression made it almost inescapable. The 'whys' and 'wherefores' of this development will be discussed further in the following section.

CLASS STRUCTURE, INDUSTRIAL RELATIONS AND THE PEACE PRESERVATION LAW

Long before the society's descent into the *'kurai tanima'* (dark valley) of the 1930s and 1940s, the antipathy between organised labour and the 'theocratic patriarchalist' *Rechtsstaat* had become clear with the publication of the Peace Preservation Law of 1900. This took place despite the existence of a new, constitutional right to freedom of association and the then current but temporary weakening of the ideology's hegemonic position. In other words, the antipathy remained one whose roots were deeply embedded in the structure of the social formation. This was an embeddedness that had hardly been disturbed by the emergence of capitalism's classes, the tensions between them and the struggles between those who embodied them. Indeed developments on the latter two fronts were such as to further strengthen the state's antipathy towards organised labour.

In a few small- and medium-sized capitalist enterprises patriarchy was occasionally challenged by the emergence of the union and socialist movements. The number of such challenges was small and their frequency occasional, because both movements were themselves small and seldom made or could make the workplace their major focus of concern. The principal exceptions to this statement, with respect to the union movement, were in the merchant navy and the Tokyo printing trade where relatively high levels of unionisation were achieved. As a result, the somewhat more egalitarian contractualist ideology associated with collective bargaining displaced the apparently spontaneously present patriarchy (Scalapino 1983). Otherwise, unions, like the various left wing political parties, were mainly and understandably concerned to secure either the political right to exist or, more desperately, to overturn completely the system that denied them that right. For this reason their interventions in the workplace tended to be occasional and short-lived (for some exceptions that prove this rule, see the case studies discussed in Scalapino 1983: 216 ff. and Totten 1974). Thus patriarchal discourse remained if not entirely intact then still very much in the ascendancy in the vast majority of small- and medium-size workplaces. Scalapino quotes one organiser as follows:

> Concerning the treatment accorded to us by working people...we have a bitter story to tell. Accustomed as they were to servile life for a long period, the material and mental advancement offered by the labor movement proves to them to be an unattractive program. To contribute one cent toward the maintenance of the movement is, they take it, a mere waste. To them, demanding of their employers their rightful share of production, is something unholy to attempt. Evils of child labour and long working hours are incomprehensible to them. It is quite natural for these people to assume an indifferent attitude toward our movement.... There are long, long years to come that we must spend in converting these people, and when we happen to think of it, our hearts lose considerable enthusiasm.
>
> (Scalapino 1983: 22)

Turning now to the rate of unionisation in large-scale enterprises, with the exception of some publicly-owned ones in the transport and utilities industries, where it reached 33 per cent and 85 per cent respectively, it was even lower than elsewhere: 5.7 per cent as opposed to an average rate of 7.5 per cent in 1933 (Taira 1970: 144–51). As in the industrialised world as a whole during the interwar period, the major long-term consequence of structural changes in large-scale enterprises was the appearance of increasing numbers of contradictory positionings on both sides of the boundary between the proletarian and capitalist classes. The largest number of such sets of positionings involved the bundling of routine managerial responsibilities (i.e. certain capitalist ideological and political positionings) with economically unambiguously proletarian positionings (for an outline of what happened in Japan, see Hirschmeier and Yui 1981: pt 3). The net effect was the beginning of a process whereby the relations between those positioned by the working class has tended to be destructured.

In Japan, as elsewhere, this development was in the postwar period to disorganise further a proletariat whose embodiments were anyway faced by a particularly divergent set of conditions, as in the same movement it increased the numbers of those who were particularly susceptible to interpellation by patriarchal ideology. What is more, this occurred in the sector of the economy that otherwise produced the conditions that made workers most resistant to such interpellation. This said, in the prewar period this section of the labour force was very small: its existence as a conduit whereby patriarchal discourse entered larger-scale workplaces in the interwar period pales into insignificance when compared to the personnel policies adopted in them in relation to the rank and file of the workforce. This was so not least because the latter policies in many ways anticipated the techniques that were to be used in the postwar period to gain and retain the loyalty of the proletariat, as well as of the 'middle-class', and which have contributed so significantly to the reproduction of the postwar period's secularised and sociologised form of patriarchy (see p.86).

Before these policies are described, some attention must first be paid to the economic dimension of the labour market development in order to explain why, even in the prewar period, workers in this sector may be thought likely to have been potentially particularly resistant to interpellation by patriarchal discourse. The opening two decades of the twentieth century saw a radical if not dramatic restructuring of the labour process in the larger-scale enterprises. The hitherto prevailing system of 'indirect control', involving labour-only subcontractors (*oyakata*), was replaced by a more direct system in which the former *oyakata* became foremen and their labourers (*kokata*) became employees of the firm (Gordon 1985: chs 1–3; Littler 1982: ch. 10). The survival of a large non- and small capitalist sector was eventually to prove an immense boon to the large-scale sector, as the 'dual economy' matured into a main contractor/subcontractor system wherein the former holds the whiphand over the latter. However, for most of the prewar period it was primarily a source of problems for the large-scale companies. This was because the myriad employment opportunities provided by the small-scale sector, when combined with the large-scale sector's apparently unnecessary fixation on 'low wages' (Taira 1970: pt 1), resulted in very high levels of labour turnover, regardless of macro-economic conditions (Napier 1982). For particular large enterprises this was especially expensive and disruptive in relation to skilled workers. Somewhat ironically, for capital as a whole it threatened to create conditions in which bargained, contractual relationships were the norm, along with all their attendant if, in the absence of much of a challenge from any unions, largely implicit dangers to industrial discipline.

In order to solve or prevent the occurrence of these problems, large-scale capital commenced to develop some of the personnel policies that have latterly become known as 'The Japanese Employment System' (JES). In place of patriarchal appeals for company loyalty on the basis of love of the owner and gratitude for his beneficence, there gradually appeared, and in a most unsystematic manner, a repertoire of appeals firmly based on the cash nexus. But these included, as a critical element, a denial of the workers' right to bargain that is otherwise implicit in that nexus. In this period only the *nenko joretsu* (seniority related pay) system was developed to any degree of sophistication, whilst such aspects of the postwar system as training, welfare schemes and employment security were seldom present, let alone systematically provided (Gordon 1985, *passim*; see also the discussion of Toyota in Allinson 1975, esp.: 102 ff.).

Thus neither the extent of large-scale capitalist development, nor the manner in which it occurred did anything to change or overcome the effects of the dominance of small-scale production in the labour market and so make trade union organisation any easier. Within this context, the unions, which had emerged first in the 1890s, grew more rapidly after the ending of the First World War, but never organised more than the 7.9 per cent they achieved in 1931. They found it very hard to achieve a breakthrough in private large-scale industry and therefore gain the strategic vantage point they sought. The strikes that their organisational efforts involved or led to, plus the opportunities these sometimes provided for anarchists, communists or other anti-*kokutai* forces, made them the principal objects of police surveillance and harassment (Ayusawa 1966; Large 1972a; 1972b; Scalapino 1983).

Again, certain ongoing political and ideological developments, such as the arrival of party cabinets, a form of manhood suffrage, and the appearance of a variety of left wing movements and political parties suggested the possibility that economic divisions might be repeated politically and ideologically, and produce thereby the possibility of a distinct consciousness amongst the embodiments of the proletariat. In the event, no such consciousness materialised. Even when male workers over 25 years of age gained the vote, they overwhelmingly voted for the bourgeois-led parties on the basis of regional, sectoral and personal loyalties. Thus the weakening of *tennosei*'s grip on the society during the 1920s, whilst obviously owing much to political and economic developments, failed to mature into any kind of ideological crisis, let alone one that could eventuate in its displacement by a more pluralistic ideological formation. This is the reason *tennosei* remained available for deployment in relation to inter-class tensions and continued to have a pre-emptive effect in relation to struggles between those who embodied the two sets of class positionings. Nothing that happened within the law itself, within *tennosei*, or within the other tectonically pertinent but relatively autonomously developing conditions of existence of the capitalist class structure did much to diminish this effect. Within this largely unchallenged and authoritarian framework, little support could be found for the extension to the parties involved in industrial relations, let alone those in dispute, of that equality of standing and privacy that is normally thought to be inherent in 'the rule of law'.

As regards the individual employment relation, this was considered in Kawashima's words to be:

a 'please let me work for you' and 'I humbly receive my wages' relationship... [And to attempt to assert one's rights was considered to be an instance of] improperly seeking relief from political authority.

(Stevens and Takahashi 1975: 124, 128)

For this reason, then, the state had little choice, as well as little hesitation, when it sought additional legal powers to those present in the criminal law in order to secure industrial discipline. It therefore increased its own police power by the passage of the Peace Preservation Law in 1900 and subsequent amendments and the formation of the Special Higher Police (the 'thought police') in 1911. The two critical articles of the Law were numbers 17 and 36, whose content Nakamura (1962: 105–61) gives as follows:

Article 17 stated that: no person can perform an act of violence, intimidation or public criticism against another person with the objects stipulated in the following clauses, nor can tempt or instigate another person with the object stipulated in clause 2.

1. No person may make another person participate or prevent him from participating in an organization engaged in cooperative activity concerning working conditions or wages.
2. No person may force an employer to discharge a worker or to refuse an application for being engaged for work or to suspend work or to refuse an application for employment as a worker with the object of carrying out a general strike or discharge.
3. No person may force another to accept the [sic] working conditions or wages

No person may commit an act of violence, intimidate or publicly criticise another in order to force him to accept the conditions of lease of land for cultivation.

Article 30 stated that a person who violates Article 17 shall be punished with penal servitude for more than one month and less than six months, with additional fines ranging from three yen to thirty yen. (For the other articles of the law and its subsequent history, see Beer 1984: ch. 2;

for statistics relating to the use of the law in strike situations, see Garon 1987: 252; and for a detailed discussion of the law and its history see Mitchell 1976).

As one would expect on the basis of the material already provided, the Law was little needed until the ending of the First World War. Even then strikes appear to have been tolerated most often (compare appendices I and III in Garon 1987) and allowed to run their course despite the presence of unions that were, if no longer illegal in themselves, certainly without legal recognition and protection. (For the Police Bureau's reinterpretation of Article 17, which in 1919 made such toleration official policy where no 'outsiders' were involved, see Garon 1987: 51.) In addition certain sections of the state bureaucracy evinced great faith in conciliation (*chotei*) as a *tennosei* alternative to repression as well as to collective bargaining. (For the struggle between supporters of repression and of the conciliatory strategy of labour control within the bureaucracy, see Garon 1987 *passim*.)

The major instances of commitment to the conciliatory faith were: passage of the Factory Law of 1911 and its revision in 1923, which provided some protection for women and children in regard of hours of employment and for all workers in regard of health and safety; the establishment of the education and research oriented Kyochokai (Harmonisation Society) with state support and finance in 1919; the passage of the Labour Disputes Conciliation Law in 1926, which repealed Article 17 of the Peace Preservation Law and replaced it with voluntary access to conciliation machinery for private industries and compulsory referral for public industries; and, finally, the *de facto* recognition of unions represented by the practice of consulting with them in relation to the welfare aspects of industrial policy and culminating in allowing union members and officials to sit as members of conciliation committees.

The judgement that the repressive and conciliatory strategies were two sides of the same coin – patriarchal state supervision rather than legally-mediated private discipline – is graphically supported by the fact that before and after the passage of the conciliation law the police were the typical agents of 'conciliation'. The inverted commas are necessary because most often, although not always, they were present either of their own

64

volition or because of a request from an employer alone, and because neither party was genuinely free to accept or reject the recommendations made by the police (Scalapino 1983: 53). The authoritarianism latent within the strategy as a whole became manifest in the 1930s as the proportion of disputes involuntarily 'conciliated' increased, reaching 75 per cent in 1935, and as the proportion conducted by the police also increased from 24 per cent in 1930 to 62 per cent in 1936. (For the same development as regards tenancy disputes, see Scalapino 1983: 224 ff.). Appropriately, some Japanese scholars have termed the strategy that so emerged 'sabre mediation' (Garon 1987: 207). In other words, it prefigured, as well as helped to prepare the ground for, the final prohibition of strikes and the suppression of unions. This commenced with the military's ban on unions in munitions plants in 1936 and culminated in 1939 in the incorporation into the state of the nazi-inspired 'industrial patriotic units' established in all factories a year earlier (Garon 1987: ch. 6). Thus in the context of the eventual disappearance of those economic, political and ideological conditions that appeared to have favoured democratic development, the disintegrative effects of the appearance of manifest social and industrial conflict in the late and post-Meiji eras were sufficient only to stimulate a desire on the part of the state and its ideologues for the police power necessary to suppress the threat to the *Kokutai*. These strikes represented to them a threat of considerably more moment than any that the same strikes represented in relation to the rights and powers of capital.

CONCLUSION

The questions that structure this study may now be answered for the second time. First, the law in the form of police power took an increasing interest in industrial relations as changing social conditions and class relations allowed unions to appear and particularly as industrial conflict took on political overtones. Second, what legitimated this interest, and what assured the success of any prosecutions that might result was the incoherence of the Civil Code and the passage and subsequent amendment of the Peace Preservation Law. Third, the eventual result of this strategy, given the effectiveness of its repressive and 'conciliatory' means of enforcement, was to maintain the repressive character of Japanese law as applied to labour and in the end to restore the disciplinary and class balances to where they had been before the emergence of unions and working-class political parties.

In the end, then, it was the rise of police power (i.e. the legal strengthening of the prerogatives of the state) that aborted the birth of a labour law premissed, like that of Britain and the United States, on the legal toleration of unions. Even the embryo of such toleration which appeared in the 1920s, did so only on the say so of the police. Thus its fate, following the onset of the Depression, should not surprise us. The proximate cause, then, for the survival of Japan's repressive labour law system is the same as that which explains the weakness of the law more generally. In a single phrase, it is 'the survival of *tennosei*'. The continued existence of *tennosei* prevented the establishment of a legal system premissed on a single principle such as the primacy of capitalist right. In the absence of the commitment to juridical consistency that is basic to 'the rule of law', the legally uncontested return of an unalloyed absolutism and a literal ideological familialism that had always been a possibility actually occurred.

Part II

POSTWAR SOCIETY AND THE RELUCTANT RECOGNITION OF LABOUR

3

FROM DEMOCRATISM TO *KIGYOSHUGI*: THE CHANGING SOCIAL CONTEXT OF LABOUR LAW

As in Part I, three questions structure what follows: (1) Why and under what circumstances did the law enter industrial relations in postwar Japan? (2) How was it that the leading cases had the outcomes they did? (3) What were the disciplinary effects of the legal outcomes on the conditions which gave rise to the leading cases? In contrast to previous chapters, where these questions were answered together in a final section, these questions will be answered separately in this and subsequent chapters because of the greater length of the answers. In the conclusion to the study as a whole and in the light of all the answers to such questions presented herein, I will return to the question of the significance of the absence of a period of toleration in the history of Japan's labour law in order to explain why Japan's current system of labour law and the role it plays in the wider society are so distinctive.

Japan's defeat in the Pacific War ushered in a period of rapid social change. Once again political change preceded and over-determined socio-economic changes. Until 1952 Japan was occupied by the Allies under the very assertive leadership of the United States and the Supreme Commander, General MacArthur. In a manner that turned out to prefigure accurately the eventual significance of the reforms that accompanied the Occupation, Japan was deprived of her sovereignty for its duration and yet continued to rule herself. The Occupation authorities or SCAP (Supreme Commander Allied Powers) initiated or approved all the major pieces of legislation, including the 'New Constitution' (Quigley and Turner 1956; Ward 1957) and the *Trade Union Law* of 1946, which for the first time granted full legality to trade unions (Gould 1984: ch.1). However, all of them were debated and passed by the Diet, promulgated by the *tenno*, implemented by the state bureaucracy, administered by the courts and enforced by the Japanese police force. Moreover, until 1947, all of these institutions continued to operate more or less as they had done under militaristic absolutism and with the same personnel.

Taking the longer view, despite the initial hostility of the Communist Party and some continuing reservations on the part of the political right, the Occupation reforms were accommodated by Japanese society, which changed in some ways but was by no means totally transformed. This was very much the case with respect to the fate of Occupation's labour legislation. However, as in Part I, an understanding of labour's changed relation to the law and of the particular structural accommodation it instances requires the prior specification of the social–structural context within which this occurred.

THE 'NEW CONSTITUTION': AMBIGUITIES OF SOVEREIGNTY

The Constitutional changes were considered by the *Diet* as if they were simply a series of amendments to the Meiji Constitution. Most subsequent scholarly comment has considered this to have been a subterfuge forced upon the *Diet* by the Occupation authorities who were anxious to find a way around the commitment, made as part of the Potsdam Declaration of 1945, that the Japanese people should be free to choose their own postwar constitution. Whether or not any anxiety existed as to how the Japanese might use any such freedom (i.e. following a socialist course), and there certainly seem to be grounds for this anxiety (Ward 1957: 648), the answer to the question as to how the constitutional changes that were made may most accurately be described is, I think, less obvious than is generally supposed. In other words, the text may still be read as signifying something of what was signified by the Meiji Constitution, despite the following differences: the claims to democratism explicitly made in the preamble; the insertion of a new Chapter II (the 'peace clause'); the deletion of many provisions that had been restrictive of individual liberty; the addition of several explicitly liberal–democratic rights; and, finally, the supremacy of an elected Diet over the executive.

The preamble was ostensibly written from the point of view of a sovereign people supposedly anxious to enjoy the very Christian and American sounding 'blessings of liberty'. Yet, the order in which the writers of the Constitution 'chose' to set out the basis upon which they proposed to pursue such enjoyment was to all intents and purposes the same as that earlier determined by the *tenno*. The significance of this is that Chapter I still defines the position and powers of the *tenno* and would still have been followed by a listing of 'the rights and duties of the people', were it not for the rather clumsily inserted 'peace clause', whose presence at this point makes the Occupation's 'arm-twisting' almost palpable. The *tenno*'s position is defined as that of 'the symbol of the State and of the unity of the people, deriving his position from the will of the people, with whom resides sovereign power'. However, the discursive ordering of the document may be read as undermining this somewhat by prompting a series of questions: Should not the nature and the rights of the sovereign (ie. 'the people') have been specified before those of their 'symbol'? Can a sovereign *qua* sovereign have duties imposed upon it and if so who or what could impose them and would not he, she or it in fact be the sovereign?

In response to the first question a positive answer seems called for, since otherwise, as with the Meiji Constitution, it appears that rights are granted by, and that duties are owed to, the *tenno*. This said, and responding to the second question, there need be no conflict between what we know the 'New Constitution' was intended to say about the location of sovereignty and what its ordering might suggest, provided that the identity of the sovereign is not in doubt. The idea that the people as sovereign may impose duties upon themselves as subjects is basic to liberal–democratic political philosophy and, therefore, if the sovereign and the people are unambiguously one and the same there is no problem. This is not the case here. The *tenno* is not defined simply as 'the symbol of the people' but as 'the symbol of the State *and* of the unity of the people' (emphasis added). According to liberal–democratic thought, the state *is* the unity of the people. Thus to distinguish the two concepts, as is done here and as is emphasised by the use of the capital 'S' in 'State', suggests that a basic law that may be read in other than liberal–democratic ways was promulgated in the New Constitution. Specifically, it suggests: (1) that the state is distinguishable from

71

and is in some sense co-sovereign with the people; (2) that, therefore, it too can grant rights and impose duties in its own interest; and (3) that the traditional distinction between the state and 'the great treasure' was still operative albeit in a somewhat qualified way. This, then, is the source of the ambiguity that makes it possible that the New Constitution might still signify something of what the Meiji Constitution signified by way of the superiority of the state *vis-à-vis* the citizenry.

That the government and some *Diet* members, at least, were aware of this ambiguity and of its latent ideological significance is clear from the following summary of part of the House of Representatives' debate on the Constitution:

> By far the most absorbing questions were those of the meaning and future locus of sovereignty, which were closely entwined with others relating to the national structure and the position of the dynasty. Hara Fujiro, *Shimpoto*, invited Mr. Kanamori [the minister responsible, A.W.] to disentangle from one another the conceptions that sovereignty resided in the state, that it belonged to the people, and that the Emperor was a participant in sovereignty as one of the people. Kanamori responded that 'if the word "sovereignty" is to be taken as the source from which the will of the state is actually derived.... I think it right to answer that in Japan 'sovereignty', without any doubt, resides in the whole people, including the Emperor'. He continued: 'Mr. Hara wanted to know in what part of the draft Constitution, then, that connotation was provided for. That is not written in so many words in the draft Constitution. That is because in Japan the Emperor and the people are one, the whole people being bound together through the spiritual ties with the Emperor which are deep-rooted in the bottom of their hearts, and this union constitutes the foundation of the existence of the state. This fact requires no explanation'.
>
> (Quigley and Turner 1956: 133; see also pp. 151 ff.)

As it has turned out, the ambiguity as to the location of sovereignty and the sense of historical continuity that this has preserved have provided the principal bases upon which it has proved possible to establish a secularised and reconstructed form of *tennosei* in the context of the rule of law – 'secularised' because the *tenno* repudiated his 'divinity' in the Imperial Rescript of 1 January 1946; 'reconstructed' because it has had to accommodate the changes forced by the democratisation that the Occupation set in train.

AMBIGUOUS FREEDOMS

Turning now to the more narrowly legal and political significance of the passage of the New Constitution, it sought to establish new freedoms and a more thoroughly democratic social structure. The Occupation powers' immediate repeal of all the most outrageously repressive laws, including the Peace Preservation Act, its reigning in and reform of the police and its grant of the franchise to women, were all followed up in the Constitution by the promulgation of rights to the classical liberal freedoms, which were extended to include the 'right of workers to organise and to bargain and act collectively', and to some Marshallian 'social rights': for example, to 'minimum standards of wholesome and cultured living', to 'the promotion and extension of social welfare and security, and of public health', to an 'equal education correspondent to their ability'.

Significant though the enhancements of freedom and the support for democratic values consequent upon the promulgation of these rights undoubtedly were and are, it is nevertheless necessary to point out that the chapter wherein they are set down contains its own echoes of the Meiji Constitution. These echoes include: the provisions of Chapter III which insist in one way or another that, in the words of Article 12, 'the people shall refrain from any abuse of these freedoms...and shall always be responsible for utilising them for the public welfare'. In contrast to the Meiji Constitution, the possibility of restrictions on these freedoms and rights is not stated directly, except in relation to property rights and, surprisingly, the freedom of abode and occupation. Rather it is present in the interpretive convention which requires all Articles to be read in the light of one another. When made explicit and articulated with the *tennosei* elements latent within Chapter I, these echoes have in fact turned out to have had restrictive consequences not only for the actual extent of democratic freedoms but also, as Riesman (quoted in Nakane

1970) has pointed out, for the very meaning of the term 'democracy':

> One has to take care that one does not misinterpret what the Japanese mean by 'democracy', a word they constantly use. It does not mean social equality: the consideration, for example, shown one's equals and official superiors is not extended to those below. 'Democracy' does seem to mean a way of doing business that combines commitment and high principle with lack of factionalism and internecine conflict. People refer to organizations as 'undemocratic' if there is no harmony or consensus. Thus democracy and politics would seem antithetical.
>
> (Nakane 1970: 148 ff.)

A case in point as regards the indirectly imposed restrictions of concern here, and which has had considerable significance for labour law, is that relating to the state's responsibilities for the public welfare. Here the restrictive potential anyway and anywhere implicit in the idea of the public welfare, and which always coexists with its more often acknowledged expansive potential, was greatly enhanced by Article 27, which states that 'All people shall have the right *and* the obligation to work' (emphasis added). However, in contrast to the Meiji Constitution, the occasion for any actual restriction may no longer be the mere existence of law allowing it, since such a law must itself pass the public welfare test. This test is administered by a Supreme Court which, thanks to Article 81 and its grant of the power of judicial review, is now the guardian of the Constitution. For example, the ultimate justification for any restrictions on freedoms or rights can no longer be simply the respect due to the *tenno*-state but must be instead a secular rationale, which must take into account such freedoms and rights as the Constitution grants. That this rationale, as it has evolved, has gained an increasingly conservative inflexion, despite or perhaps because of the Court's reluctance to use its power of judicial review, is the consequence of the Liberal Democratic Party's successes in postwar electoral contests, as well as of the not unrelated continuing power of the state bureaucracy. To put the point another way, what the courts might have come to regard as the public welfare and hence what they might have come to allow in the way of secondary industrial citizenship would in all likelihood have been very different had the Japan Socialist Party (JSP) also held power for any length of time.

As provided in Chapter IV of the Constitution, the Diet remained a bicameral chamber, except that both houses were to contain elected members only and the upper-house was re-named the House of Councillors. Additionally, as provided in Chapter V, executive power was unambiguously vested in a cabinet chosen and led by a Prime Minister and responsible only to a Diet elected on the basis of a universal franchise. This Diet was given the power to reject all measures placed before it, including the budget. It would serve no purpose here to go over in any detail the outcomes of the numerous general and intra-party elections that have been held since 1947 (for analyses as well as the details, see Curtis 1988; Stockwin 1982). Suffice it to say that, despite the fact that the first prime minister under the New Constitution was a socialist, all the subsequent holders of the office have led either coalitions of conservative parties or, since 1955, the Liberal Democratic Party (LDP) which grew out of these coalitions.

All that has varied are the size of the conservative majority and the ideological and programmatic bases upon which the parties have appealed to the electorate. These variations are significant for two major reasons, both of which suggest that the content of the conservatism that had been hegemonic during the postwar period has not been unchanging. First, because they indicate that the general social balance, if not the location, of political and, by extension, ideological power has changed somewhat over time. Second, because in response to the striking reduction in the size of the LDP's majority in the latter half of the 1970s, which undermined the claimed 'naturalness' of its rule, the party was forced to develop a policy-making capacity that was independent of the bureaucracy (Curtis 1988: 106 ff.). This, in turn, has had the latently very significant ideological consequence of tending to undermine the political primacy of the bureaucracy.

POSTWAR PARTY POLITICS

As a first indication of the nature of the variations of concern here, one may distinguish three different party systems in the postwar period: the first was the very fissiparious multi-party system which existed between the Surrender (1945) and 1955; the second was the so-called 'one-and-a-half party system' which existed between 1955 and 1964; and the third is the rather stable multi-party system which has existed since 1964. On the right of the political spectrum there were two major parties at the inception of the first system: the Progressives, who formed around politicians who had been active in the IRAA (Imperial Rule Assistance Association) during the war, and the Liberals, who formed around the remains of the prewar *Seiyukai*. Stimulated by SCAP's purge of 'undesirable personnel', which not surprisingly bore particularly heavily upon the Progressives, these two groupings divided and reunited in a series of kaleidoscopic shake-ups. Over the next few years they reappeared, first, as the Democrats and the Democratic–Liberals; second, as the Reformers and the Hatoyama/Yoshida Liberals; and finally, as the Democrats and the Liberals, who merged in 1955 to form the Liberal Democratic Party.

On the left the major parties at the inception of the first system were the Socialists and the Communists. The former split into separate right and left parties in 1951 and reunited again in 1955, whilst the latter crumbled following the 'red purge' of 1950–1. Throughout the time the first system was in place and indeed throughout the duration of the second system, the conservative parties received close on 60 per cent of the vote, thanks largely to the high levels of support they received from employers, the burgeoning ranks of middle-management ('salarymen') and the vast new group of small landowners created by the land reform programme. The socialists and their allies received around 30 per cent of the vote, which they owed largely to the rather lower proportions of support which they received from unionised workers and the intelligentsia (Curtis 1988: ch.6).

Ideologically, the competition between the parties of the first two systems revolved around the Constitution and the other more specific reforms introduced by the Occupation authorities. The keenest supporters of the Constitution and the reforms were the socialists, whose ability to maintain their grip on around one third of the seats in the Diet after the Occupation came to an end ensured that no drastic alterations were made. The influence of the socialists was maintained despite the fact that the Occupation authorities had increasingly come to favour the conservatives. The beginning of the latter process was SCAP's decision to ban the general strike called for February 1947 (Moore 1983). Its progress was marked by such developments as the decision to withdraw the rights to organise and/or to strike from public service workers in 1948 (see pp.113–16) and the adoption of the programme of economic austerity known, after the banker who designed it, as 'the Dodge Line'. In the deepening shadow of the Cold War, its culmination came with the 'red purge' and the signing of the peace and mutual security treaties between Japan and the United States in 1952, which ended the Occupation and allowed, even encouraged, the partial and informal revocation of the Constitution's peace clause.

Once the Occupation ended, the then conservative government and its successors commenced what the opposition called 'the reverse course'. This centred on the following areas: police administration and powers, union rights, educational administration and content, defence and the Constitution. The police were re-centralised, but gained no additional formal powers. The rights of employees in the coal and electricity industries were restricted but the rights of employees in general were not. The educational system was re-centralised and the Ministry of Education gained the power to vet and authorise textbooks, as well as to insist upon the teaching of 'ethics' in schools. The 'peace clause' of the Constitution was violated by the establishment of the 'Self-Defence Forces', and the Mutual Security Treaty with the United States was renegotiated, in both cases despite very strong protest campaigns by the left. Finally, a cabinet commission was established to review the Constitution.

The limited nature of the reversals that were attempted, let alone of those that were achieved, suggests that the society was in fact settling around a new centre of ideological gravity during what is otherwise most often presented as simply a period of sharp polarisation. This is a reading the plausibility of which is further enhanced when one recalls that this period also saw the onset of the decline in support for the Socialist Party and the occurrence of the split that created the small Democratic Socialist Party in 1959. The JSP's decline began around the time that it became clear that the gradualist, 'structural reform' faction would lose its anyway rather tenuous grip on the party leadership (Curtis 1988: 138–48). The specification of the nature of this centre of ideological gravity and of its conditions of existence must wait until the economic developments of the period, which were what underpinned it, have been outlined.

In the meantime, the present section will conclude by suggesting that with hindsight it is possible to argue that the nature and the balance of forces apparent under the new multi-party system that emerged in the mid-1960s confirms the existence of a more or less 'still centre' amidst the swirling eddies of everyday factional politics. At the time, however, a very different reading seemed at least equally plausible. The mid-1960s saw the emergence of two parties, the buddhist Komeito party (Curtis 1988: 24–7; White 1970) and a revived Communist Party (Curtis 1988: 27–30), both committed in their very different ways to assuaging the fears and pressing the demands of particular urban social groups – i.e. small businesspeople, service workers and non-unionised workers in small factories – all of whom justifiably felt that they were not sharing fully in the fruits of the economic 'miracle'. Like the Socialist Party but with less ambivalence, both parties offered fully-fledged alternatives to the ideological *status quo*. However, although they gained support very rapidly, the 10 per cent share of the vote that they had each attained by the early 1970s turned out to indicate the presence of a rather definite ceiling to their possible levels of support – a ceiling that was reinforced by the flexibility that the LDP demonstrated in responding to the different but related concerns of its own increasingly urban, middle-class supporters.

Through the widespread urban citizens' movements of the early to mid-1970s, the ideological challenge spread as some of the middle-class beneficiaries of 'the miracle' found a common cause with those who felt excluded, and as together they created their own, non-party agenda (pollution, land prices, municipal services, etc.), which revolved around the general theme of 'the quality of life'. At the national level, the same theme recurred in demands for improved welfare and health programmes, as well as for enhanced opportunities for access to higher education. Thus the discovery of the myopia and fallibility of the local state was combined with a certain disillusionment with the national state, which additionally seemed to be making unexpectedly heavy weather of the various 'shocks' (revaluation of the yen, the United States' new China policy, the oil price rise) of the early 1970s. (For the Lockheed scandal that brought down Prime Minister Tanaka and the associated 'discovery' of 'money politics', see Johnson 1986; Woronoff 1986: 314 ff.) The net result was a loosening of party loyalties, which resulted in the LDP losing its absolute majority in the House of Representatives for the first time in 1976.

Nevertheless the LDP continued to form the government with the support of the New Liberal Club which had only recently split from it. In addition, the ruling party's factional structure, which largely reflects the financial exigencies created by the multi-member constituency structure rather than ideological differences (Curtis 1988, pp. 80–8, 179–83; Stockwin 1982: 35–8), enabled it to be more responsive to the political possibilities inherent in the emergence of what might be called 'Middle Japan' than the ideologically factionalised and therefore politically less flexible Socialist Party. Thus, when in the early 1980s the concerns of Middle Japan somewhat belatedly began to centre on what high levels of inflation could do to their savings, which because of the high land prices tends to take a monetary rather than the bricks and mortar form common in Britain and the United States, the LDP was able to respond far more quickly than the opposition parties. Moreover, by taking a leaf out of Mrs Thatcher's book, the LDP found, through the privatisation of the telecommunications, railway and tobacco industries, a way of making reductions in state expenditure doubly profitable to many of its supporters: privatisation allowed taxes to be kept low and enabled capital assets to be distributed more widely than they otherwise might have been. Even if they had wanted to, the opposition parties would have found it hard to respond in the same way, since their often unionised and public sector supporters had most to lose as a result of privatisation and decreased government spending, and, because of their lower levels of savings, least to lose as a result of any inflation.

In the 1986 election, the restored health and vitality of the economy, dramatised by the growing and not always very deeply regretted 'trade friction' with much of the rest of the world, enabled the LDP to regain, if not the 60 per cent share of the vote it had formerly received, a 50 per cent share that made it once again clearly the majority party. However, a significant percentage of the support upon which this majority depends, now appears to depend upon a substantive calculation on the part of the LDP's urban and middle-class constituency that the party's reading of the political runes may be worth something tangible to them as individuals (Curtis 1988, 200 ff.). However, the basis upon which the party does its reading has become less and less distinctively its alone, as the opposition parties and especially the JSP have come to share the view, albeit slowly and often grudgingly, that there is something distinctively and valuably Japanese about the way in which the economic success of the postwar period was achieved.

POSTWAR ECONOMIC DEVELOPMENT

As with the development of the polity, three phases may be distinguished in that of the economy: a first phase of recovery (1945–55); a second phase of high economic growth (1956–70); and a third and more troubled phase of maturity (1970–), as European and American commentators comfortingly term it. Recovery was slow to begin for a number of reasons: the devastation caused by the war was immense; overseas assets and markets had disappeared, as had the merchant fleet; the value of domestic assets was hugely diminished by inflation; companies, especially large ones, were fearful of the Occupation authorities' wrath in the light of what they knew to be its analysis of the roots of Japanese expansionism, namely economic imperialism; and, finally, these fears proved to be justified, since the Occupation authorities' interest in the economy for the first two years was marked by an overwhelming concern to destroy the basis of this imperialism. Thus it not only pushed for constitutional and other non-economic reforms, but it also made a serious effort to restructure the economy and alter its wider societal impact by making it a source of support for democracy rather than allowing it to remain its antithesis. In this connection, the most important Occupation measures were the dissolution of the *zaibatsu* and the purging of many of their senior personnel, the virtual abolition of agricultural landlordism (Dore 1959), the passage of rigorous anti-trust legislation, and the passage of the aforementioned series of labour and welfare laws that promised to redress the prewar balance in the workplace and the labour market (Allen 1965: ch. 2).

The immediate result of all this was almost complete economic paralysis, as capital struck in protest and as labour failed to obtain the political primacy and the raw materials necessary to recommence production on its own behalf (Moore 1983). Very quickly the mounting cost of this paralysis to the American taxpayer and the dangers espied in labour's response to it forced a rethink on the part of the Occupation authorities that led to the formulation of 'The Dodge Line' in 1948. None of the economic reforms were rescinded but equally, with the possible and from the LDP's point of view the politically portentous exception of land reform, all were qualified in one way or another by the way in which they were put into practice. Once the Occupation authorities had firmly decided on a capital rather than a labour-organised economic recovery, once overseas trade recommenced and so allowed the import of fuel and raw materials, and once the Korean War began, the economy revived very quickly. By 1951 industrial production exceeded its prewar level and every year thereafter similar successes were recorded until in 1955, with real GNP 55 per cent above its prewar level, the recovery process may be said to have come to an end.

Thereafter, with the odd break caused, as in the earlier period, by balance of payments deficits, the economy continued to grow spectacularly with an average growth rate of just over 12 per cent. The reasons for this growth need not be gone into here (but see, Denison and Chung 1976; Friedman 1988; Johnson 1982). Suffice it to say that they revolve around what was in comparative terms the very effective use of what were initially very scarce capital resources. Rapidly increasing state and company revenues, supplemented by competitive and responsive bank-lending and undiminished by military or welfare obligations and high taxes, were invested in a complementary manner in shrewdly or fortuitously chosen industries – industries which prospered behind high tariff barriers and yet, thanks to the undervalued yen, were able to find ready markets for their increasingly high value-added products in an ever more open and somewhat complacent world economy (Allen 1965; Patrick and Rosovsky 1976; Yamamura 1967). Although one must not forget that it cannot be understood in isolation from the factors just mentioned, and indeed would not have been possible in their absence, there seems to be no reason to demur from the general agreement with the argument advanced by Patrick and Rosovsky (1976: 94) that the critical and, in a sense, synthetic factor was the skilful, or perhaps, again, fortuitous, way in which imported and, by Japanese standards, highly advanced technology and foreign patents were combined with indigenous labour.

The term 'fortuitous' was used above because the manner in which this combinatory activity was organised certainly owed something, and perhaps a great deal, to certain at first glance rather awkward socio-economic factors about which corporate management could do little and which it had to find a way around. Thus the achievement of such management is not so much that it dreamt up new ways of doing things, inspired by some brilliant and exotic thought, as is suggested in much of the popular management literature, but rather that it responded rationally, creatively and sometimes ruthlessly (e.g. where labour was concerned, see p.150 and Halberstam 1986: ch. 26) to the situation that confronted it in the sphere of production. The particular structural circumstance that gave an especially distinctive quality to the background, against which any decision had to be made as to how labour and capital should be combined, was the continuing vitality of small business and the consequently continuing 'dualism' of its industrial structure (Chalmers 1989).

The most commented upon industrial policies of the postwar era all benefited large-scale industry far more obviously and directly than they benefited smaller scale concerns. The policies I have in mind here are especially: the establishment of, and the funding and the administrative guidance offered by, the Ministry of International Trade and Industry (see Johnson 1982); the associated reform and relaxation of anti-trust policy in relation to the reconstruction of the industrial–financial combines (*Keiretsu*); and the encouragement of capital-intensive industries such as heavy engineering and latterly micro-electronics. Throughout the first two phases of postwar development such policies were often justified on the basis that, apart from anything else, they would result in a dramatic shrinking of the exploited and exploiting small-scale sector. Even before the end of the second phase, it was clear that no such result had occurred (Broadbridge 1966: ch. 3). Nor has it occurred since, although there are reasons for thinking that under the current boom conditions the relationship is no longer always quite as exploitative as it was (Friedman 1988). In 1982, enterprises employing under 100 workers provided jobs for 68.7 per cent of the labour force, those employing under 30 for 56.4 per cent and those employing under 5 for 30.6 per cent. Agriculture and fisheries have a massive preponderance of enterprises employing less than 30 people, whilst in the construction and distribution sectors roughly two-thirds and in the service and manufacturing sectors roughly one-third of the enterprises are of such a size (Patrick and Rohlen 1987: 339).

Undoubtedly, there are positive reasons for the continuing vitality of the small business sector. These have to do with the survival of traditional crafts, the allure of economic independence in an otherwise extremely conformist and hierarchical society, the possibility of financial success, and the desire to hold on to the valuable patrimony that the postwar land reform distributed widely amongst once rural, but now often suburban and even urban populations (Patrick and Rohlen 1987: 363 ff.). For such reasons, alongside a low and lax tax regime, the absence of unions and the inapplicability of, or half-hearted enforcement of, the Labour Standards Law (Chalmers 1989: 101–5), one may readily see why there should be a substantial body of independent entrepreneurs. However, as Patrick and Rohlen have emphasised, such reasons do not explain why such entrepreneurs should so readily find an even more substantial body of very able employees, who are willing to work for what are usually lower wages and under worse conditions than those enjoyed by their equivalents in larger companies. To explain the presence of such employees one has to look beyond narrow economic factors. On the negative side, there exists widespread and deeply-rooted discrimination against women, Japanese-born minorities (Burakumin, Ainu, Okinawans, Koreans), older people and, most recently, 'illegal workers' from such countries as Bangladesh, Pakistan and the Philippines (Patrick and Rohlen 1987: 358 ff.; see also Chalmers 1989: ch. 3; Lee and De Vos 1981; Hingwan 1990). Additionally, not only have the opportunities for work in large companies ceased to grow as quickly as they once did (Koshiro 1985), but also state welfare provision has remained meagre in spite of the improvements of the 1970s. On the positive side, the education system and the socialisation process more generally have ensured that the labour force as a whole is capable of disciplined and highly skilled work.

Given these conditions and the growing availability of capital for small enterprises, large companies have been able to concentrate their resources on the development, assembly and sale of products comprising parts provided by subcontractors, with confidence in both the quality of the parts and the subcontractors' capacity to respond to variations in demand and changes in specifications, and without having to attempt to buck established prejudices. Thus although, with the collusion of their unions, the large companies initially reinforced the discriminations that they took advantage of, in the end, thanks to the considerable and skilfull attention they paid to the refinement of production techniques and such related logistical skills as those represented by the 'just in time' inventory control system (*kanban*), they became part of an immensely strengthened, still dualistic but in some ways less obviously stratified economic system. As it turned out, this system was increasingly capable of just the kind of 'flexible specialisation' (Piore and Sabel 1984) that proved to be one of the keys to economic success during the 1970s and 1980s.

This flexibility has become ever more the hallmark of the economy as its participants have struggled (sometimes with one another) to respond to the difficulties of the last two decades. These were difficulties that saw the economy slow down to an average growth rate of 7.5 per cent for the period 1970–3 and to one of 3.8 per cent for the period 1974–85. They were also difficulties that saw the revenues of large companies cease to expand as quickly as before, because of the increased capital costs associated with a growing need to engage in massive but no longer so productivity-enhancing plant renewal programmes, and because of the increased labour costs caused by the rising expectations of their labour force, voiced and enforced by their employees' increasingly united unions in a situation of tightening labour supply. Finally, these were difficulties that, despite a significant tightening of the legal framework within which unions operate which began in the early 1970s, saw capital's room to manoeuvre in relation to these developing constraints dramatically reduced. This reduction was brought about by the oil and currency shocks of 1973, which pushed up costs yet again and made it harder still for companies to 'export' themselves and the country out of trouble.

Despite all these problems and because of the 'flexible rigidities' (Dore 1986; Friedman 1988) that have become the economy's major assets, the growth rate of the Japanese economy nevertheless remained two or three times that of its competitors throughout the 1970s. This difference was sustained into the 1980s thanks in large part to the United States' decision to engage in massive deficit-spending. This allowed a new Japanese export boom, this time in capital (to finance the US deficit) as well as in the other commodities for which Japan used to be better known (Lincoln 1988; Yamamura and Yasuba 1987). Notwithstanding the economic slow-down and the occasional media panics that have accompanied it, this relative and enviable success has had the important domestic consequence of sustaining the claims to economic superiority, which have been central to the hegemonic ideology since the early 1960s and which have given credibility and substance to many of its other claims.

IDEOLOGY AFTER *TENNOSEI*

The sole condition insisted upon by the Japanese government as it negotiated surrender terms with the Allies was preservation of the national *Kokutai*.[1] This it achieved when a place was allowed to the *tenno* in the New Constitution. For most commentators this was a case of a battle won, but another war lost. The Occupation reforms and the democratisation which they set in train are generally supposed to have caused 'the prewar concept of *Kokutai* [to have] crumbled away altogether' (Gluck 1985: 284). Here, however, a contrary argument will be advanced. Namely, that the economically critical elements of *tennosei* were not so much destroyed as displaced and partially transformed. Specifically, it will be argued that the central role as the embodiment of Japan's uniqueness, hitherto played by the *tenno* was taken by that of the *ie* (the patriarchal household). Thus the hegemonic ideology was sociologised as well as secularised by the somewhat ambiguous transfer of sovereignty from the *tenno* to the people.

From the point of view of those still interpellated by a very literal reading of *tennosei*, such as the conservatives of the immediate postwar period, the ambiguities in the transfer of sovereignty had much to recommend them in what for them were desperate days, somewhat akin, in anthropological terms, to those faced by messianic cults 'when prophecy fails' (Cohn 1957). They granted some legitimacy to the arrangements fate had imposed and, in the highly ambiguous words of the *tenno*'s surrender broadcast, enabled the irreconcilables to 'endure the unendurable' – the important, almost the only point, was that the *tenno*-line remained unbroken, just as it had during the Shogunate. From the points of view of those not so interpellated – the majority it would appear (Gluck 1985: 286) – who either by conviction or out of necessity wished to take or to be seen to take the new democratism seriously, the uniqueness of their society, which only some of the communists and socialists doubted, gradually came to be seen as lying in their 'Japanese way of life'.

Respect for the *tenno* was of course an aspect, and an important one, of this way of life, but increasingly the *tenno* became, as stated in the New Constitution, its symbol rather than its essence. Thus the society appears to have experienced what might be called a 'Durkheimian revelation' concerning the relation between the sacred and the social, except that for Durkheim (1961) the discovery that in worshipping its gods a society was in fact worshipping itself destroyed the basis for religious belief as such. In postwar Japan this does not seem to have been the result. The veneration once reserved for the ancestral spirits and the *tenno* and the duties consequently owed to them was in large part transferred to such institutions as the *ie* or, more substantively following the legal demise of the *ie* (see p. 98), to the institutions and especially the *kaisha* (large companies) which supposedly embody the *ie* essence. Indeed it was noting the repetition of a certain awe if not exactly a reverence towards such institutions in everyday conversation which first suggested to me that what one is confronted with in the changing ideological structure of postwar Japan is an instance of a complex displacement rather than of a simple transformation – a displacement whereby the presently dominant sign, *ie*, was formerly a subordinate one (i.e. as an aspect of the society's 'beautiful customs'). Whereas in *tennosei* proper the *tenno* gave the society its 'beautiful customs', in its transmuted postwar form the beautiful customs first gave society its '*tenno*' and latterly gave it its *kaisha*. (The texts which best exemplify the process whereby this displacement took place in constitutional/legal discourse are those contained in the reports of the proceedings of the Commission on the Constitution which met between 1958 and 1964, see Maki 1980).

Thus far I have referred to the hegemonic postwar ideology only as a secularised and sociologised form of *tennosei* because

I wanted to stress the continuities involved. From now on, in order to be able to acknowledge the differences which have followed from what was certainly a radical even if not a revolutionary discursive reordering, I propose to use the term *Kigyôshugi* (enterprisism or belief in the intrinsic virtue of the company) to refer to it. This term recommends itself because, in identifying the Japanese company as the principal object of the hegemonic discourse, it acknowledges both the occurrence of the displacement of concern here and the exemplary as well as central role of the *kigyô* (enterprise) and more particularly the *kaisha* in the postwar reconstruction of Japanese institutions. This said, it is necessary for me to emphasise that, in opting to use the term *Kigyôshugi*, I am not saying that the company is the sole source of themes in the hegemonic discourse, but only that it is the dominant source of such themes and therefore of the interpellative means whereby the Japanese people are attached and attach themselves to their society. All of the signifiers that feature in the discourse which is hegemonic in the United States (i.e. 'self-reliance', 'responsible unionism', 'opportunity', 'loyalty' and 'modernism', see Woodiwiss 1990a: ch. 7 and 1991, *passim*) also feature in that of Japan, as indeed to a lesser degree and as oppositional currents do their more social-democratic western European equivalents. However, what these terms signify both individually and collectively in Japan is very different, thanks largely to the discursive omnipresence of 'the group', in the form of such signifiers as *kaisha* and its non-business equivalents. The core of what these significations are is what must now be explicated.

The belief that there is something unique about Japan's social arrangements and that this is crystallised in the existence of a supposedly trans-institutional *ie* form of organisation is one that appears to have established itself in Japanese academia in the mid to late 1960s. The academy remains one of the principal sites where *Kigyôshugi* is reproduced. However, it is not the only or even the most important of such sites, since the academics and the less scholarly contributors to the related and hugely popular *Nihonjinron* (theories of Japaneseness) literature (see Dale 1988) have made their contributions as a result of reflecting upon what appears to them to be going on at other sites. Nor, of course, are the non-academics whom the ideology additionally interpellates necessarily aware of believing in anything called a 'trans-institutional *ie* form of organisation'. Rather they are so interpellated by working and living in 'industrial enterprises, government organisations, educational institutions, intellectual groups, religious communities, political parties, village communities, individual households and so on' (Nakane 1970: i), each of whose structures is constructed, or so the academics argue, on the basis of what Nakane has termed 'the vertical principle' and Murakami (1984: 309) 'homo-functional hierarchy'. Nakane elaborates as follows:

> The relationship between two individuals of upper and lower status is the basis of the structural principle of Japanese society. This important relationship is expressed in the traditional terms *oyabun* and *kobun*. *Oyabun* means the person with the status of *oya* (parent) and *kobun* means the status of *ko* (child).... The essential elements in the relationship are that the *kobun* receives benefits or help from his *oyabun*, such as assistance in securing employment or promotion, and advice on the occasion of important decision-making. The *kobun*, in turn is ready to offer his service whenever the *oyabun* requires them.
>
> (Nakane 1970: 44)

Murakami, who in addition to being hugely influential despite his recent disgrace was also a member of Prime Minister Nakasone's 'brains trust', is somewhat less metaphorical and defines two variants of the structure, which are supposedly exhaustive of virtually all significant institutional life in Japan. He suggests that the first may be found most often within single institutions, whereas, until recently at least, the second may be found most often where otherwise separate institutions are combined, as in *Keiretsu* (the financial/industrial groupings that have replaced the *zaibatsu*) and *shitauke* (main contractor/subcontractor groups):

1. The *ie* genotype is the tight version of the indigenous organisational principle and is defined as a group having the following characteristics:

a. Collective goal: eternal continuation and expansion of

the group, which is often symbolised by stem succession to group leadership.

b. Membership qualification: 'kintractship', that is, no member should leave the group once he or she joins it.

c. Hierarchy–homogeneity balance: all members are organised in a hierarchy aiming at some functional goal, and various complementary measures further their homogeneity.

d. Autonomy: the group encompasses all functions necessary to its perpetuation.

2. The *mura* variant, the loose version of the indigenous organisational principle, is defined as a group with the following characteristics:

a. Collective goal: very long term continuation and expansion of the group.

b. Membership qualification: every member should stay with the group as long as it continues.

c. Homogeneity–hierarchy balance: all members are considered to be homogeneous and therefore treated equally, but they implicitly share a sense of ranking that reflects, by and large, functional capability.

d. Multifunctionality: the group achieves and reconciles diverse interrelated functions.

(Murakami 1987: 35–6)

In 1980, these ideas surfaced as an official text, namely as a research bureau report of the Ohira cabinet entitled 'Economic administration of the age of culture'. Harootunian (1989: 80–1) has very usefully summarised the pertinent section of this report and in a way moreover that stresses the importance that is attached to mobilising precisely those 'subtler pressures exerted by *oyabun* and other kinds of bosses', which Maruyama Masao, the leading democratic intellectual of postwar Japan, regarded as so pervasive and fearful a part of Japanese society:

Japan's 'cultural particularity', which has been described as a relationalism (*aidagarashugi*) [inheres in its privileging of] the relationship between human and human, between part and whole, as expressed in words like *ningen*, 'between people', *nakama*, 'within relationships', and *seken*, 'within society'. Japanese, therefore, emphasize the importance of essence (*ki*) embedded in human relationships, and subsequently stress the centrality of one's participation in a larger complex – *bun*, as found in terms like *kibun* [feeling], *jibun* [self], *hombun* [duty], *mibun* [social position], *shokubun* [duty], etc. Discerning the quality of *bun* requires exhausting oneself in it and is thus linked to *en*, binding ties, as represented in the following relationships: *ketsu-en* [kin], *chi-en* [territorial group], *gakuen* [college], and *sha-en* [company]. All signify the characteristic of the '*nakama* society' or the '*ie* society', a social constellation held together by fundamental and culturally irreducible relationships that determine how one is to behave with reference to others within the confines of Japanese society.

(Harootunian 1989: 80–1)

The *terminus ad quem* of this line of argument as it relates to economic institutions has recently been stated with particular clarity, albeit and interestingly perhaps unconsciously, by Kuwahara:

The Japanese enterprise...should be called a 'business community maintained by labour and management', rather than a 'capitalistic enterprise' in which the sovereign power of the stockholders is predominant.

(Kuwahara 1989: 10)

What cannot be doubted, as all public pronouncements by Japanese institutions, all studies and any experience of working in them attests, is that a great deal of effort is put into making it appear that the harmony (*wa*) expected of *ie* or *mura*-type (village-type) institutions does in fact characterise them. What, equally, can only be doubted is the claim made by such as Nakane, Murakami and official company spokespeople that these efforts are wholly successful and, therefore, that contemporary Japanese institutions are in fact entirely free of the structural tensions, especially between labour and capital, that most schools of sociology, excluding structural–functionalism and some of the more bizarre forms of post-Marxism, regard as intrinsic to capitalism. As it happens, there are many signs of structural–functionalism in the texts written by such authors (e.g. they are explicit in Nakane's talk of 'shared values' and throughout the quotation from Murakami given above). However, they do not base their claims upon a commitment to any particular school of sociology, let alone one as quintessentially American as structural–functionalism. Instead they argue that their claims are based simply on observation. However, observation is never as theoretically or ideologically innocent as they appear to think, and in their case it was and remains powerfully affected by a prior commitment to a symbiotic combination of structural functionalism and the uniqueness assumption.

It is sufficient for now to repeat that *Kigyôshugi* texts such as those of Nakane and Murakami are more interesting as instances of that discourse than as guides to its understanding (see also Woodiwiss 1989). In the meantime, this section will approach its end by mentioning a suggestion made by Murakami (1987: 58 ff.) amongst others that there are grounds for thinking that the actual ideological formation may no longer correspond to the established representations of it in academic texts (hence his attention to the *mura* variant?). He correctly draws attention to the significance of the emergence of what he terms 'the new middle mass' in explaining any such development. However, what is difficult to accept is his suggestion that the element of egalitarianism he imagines to be present in *mura*-type organisations is any more real than the consensus supposedly present in the more traditional *ie*-type organisations. Whom one agrees with on this point, Murakami or the present author, depends not simply upon where one stands on the uniqueness issue, but also upon what one thinks is involved in the emergence of the new middle mass, and as will be made clear in the final chapter we have very different views on this. Nevertheless, what this development in Murakami's work suggests is the possibility that *Kigyôshugi* may be changing along with its social–structural conditions of existence. This is a development whose occurrence is also attested to by the first recurrence since the 1940s of doubts as to the omniscience of the state bureaucracy (see p. 78) and, relatedly, by the appearance of new doubts as to the inevitability of the LDP's political supremacy and the unqualified worthwhileness of economic success.

91

THE RISE OF THE LABOUR MOVEMENT

The challenge to the trade unions in the social context just outlined was to find a way of surviving once the revolutionary aspirations of some of them were disappointed, once capital had been restructured and its embodiments reorganised into its various 'peak associations' (e.g. Keidanren, Nikkeiren), and especially once the meeting of the latter's requirements had become the major preoccupation of the state. In responding to this challenge, the unions were, by turns, helped and hindered by the developing labour law in ways which will be specified in the two following chapters, as well as by developments at the level of class relations which will be specified in Chapter 6.

Two of the developments which indicated a strengthening of those positioned by the working class and which therefore may be assumed to have helped the unions in the postwar period have already been described: specifically, the leftwing parties' ability to maintain a level of Diet representation sufficient to thwart any effort at constitutional revision; and the slight but significant shift in the nature of the hegemonic discourse, which has forced some at least of those who enunciate it to allow that the lengthened hierarchies and the consequent slight dispersion of power found within *ie* and *mura*-type institutions are properly Japanese. Only the unions' own but very much related maintenance of their positions in the postwar period remains to be described.

In the midst of the postwar chaos and so in responding to urgent practical needs as well as to the new legal and political possibilities, unions formed at an incredibly rapid rate (Moore 1983). By the end of 1946 something like 3.6 million workers or 39.5 per cent of the labour force had been organised. Reflecting the exigencies of the time and in the absence of any alternative, the vast majority of the unions so formed were enterprise- rather than skill or industry-based. Many of these unions quickly formed themselves into industry federations (*tan sans*) and soon afterwards joined one or other of three confederations. These confederations were a reorganised Sodomei, which was closely related to the JSP, Sanbetsu-Kaigi (Congress of Japanese Industrial Unions), which was closely related to the JCP, and Nichiro-Kaigi (Japan Conference of Labour Unions), which was politically neutral. Until 1949 Sanbetsu was the most influential centre by virtue of a militancy that, in the context of the opening of the Cold War, turned the Occupation authorities against the labour movement, caused them to prohibit the general strike called for in February 1947 and, finally, to allow the restrictions on unions which were hurriedly introduced in 1948.

Between 1949 and 1956 and as with the political parties, a kaleidoscopic series of changes resulted in the emergence, in turn, of the socialist-led Sohyo, which displaced the still surviving Sodomei as the largest single trade union confederation, and the more moderate but still socialist-led Zenro as well as the non-political and exclusively private sector Churitsuroren as its smaller rivals. In 1956 the domestic and international political concerns that had hitherto dominated the politics of the confederations, centrally the proposed renegotiation of the United States–Japan Security Treaty, gave way to domestic economic ones as the employers took the very tough line symbolised by the Miike coalmine dispute. This line was carried forward by the companies' 'sponsorship' of more pliant 'second unions' in the context of the establishment of the JES with its principles of lifetime employment, seniority wages and enterprise unions. However, 1956 was also the year when the Sohyo-led Spring Labour Offensive (*shunto*) commenced in earnest and so gave to the Japanese industrial relations year its distinctive rhythm. Gradually the *shunto* gained the support of all the major union groupings, including the initially highly critical Zenro, which was reborn as Domei in 1964. This was because it had proved to be of some use in countering the divide-and-rule tactics institutionalised in the largely income-related forms of the early JES.

At the core of the *shunto* strategy is the agreement by all of the participants to a single set of demands, which nowadays extend beyond wage issues, and to a set of what might be termed 'rules of engagement', which specify the order (strongest first) in which unions will engage in direct conflict with the employers if the national negotiations with the employers' organisation (Nikkeiren) should require it. With the settlement norms set in this way, the *shunto* ends with enterprise level negotiations which result in agreements that vary around the norms, depending upon market and company-specific conditions. These variations can be considerable if special conditions are recognised by individual unions and the confederations to which they belong, as has been the case recently in the declining steel and shipbuilding industries, whose unions were once in the vanguard of the *shunto*. Encouraged by the success of this unified approach in both the good times of the 1960s and the more difficult times of the 1970s and 1980s, throughout which it has encountered tightening economic, ideological and legal constraints, the various confederations have sought organisational unity and greater political flexibility. These moves culminated in the creation of Rengo (The Japanese Private Sector Trade Union Confederation) in November 1987 and Sohyo's entry into it in the Autumn of 1989. Since this date the renamed Shin (new) Rengo has organised approximately two-thirds of all the organised workers in Japan. The remaining third are organised by a much smaller (1.4 million members), communist-led confederation (Zenroren) and by enterprise unions which remain unaffiliated to any centre. Perhaps significantly, since it might prefigure a wider interest in social rights, all of these federations have recently suggested that their *shunto* or *shunto*-related demands should begin to emphasise such qualitative issues as reducing working hours and increasing holidays (although I have not heard it mentioned, there would seem to be a particularly compelling case for double-time payments in relation to holiday work!).

When compared with the prewar situation, all of this represents a story of considerable achievement. However, it is important not to lose sight of the fact that, despite much of the labour movement's maintenance of a formal commitment to a revolutionary socialist ideology, this achievement has involved an accommodation with capital as well as an encroachment upon some of its traditional powers. This is suggested not only by the labour movement's lack of interest in or failure to enforce a 'system of secondary industrial citizenship' (an especially egregious failure where the rights of women, minorities and, most recently, foreign workers are concerned), but also by the fact (perhaps related, perhaps not) that the postwar period has witnessed a steady decline in the size of the organised proportion of the labour force. In 1990 only some 25 per cent of the labour force were members of trade unions of any kind, which means that Shin Rengo represents only around 20 per cent of the total labour force. This said, it is equally important to bear in mind, when attempting to assess the strength as well as the sense of social responsibility of the Japanese trade union movement, that the bulk of its membership (62.8 per cent in 1981) are employed by enterprises with 500 or more employees. It is also particularly strongly represented in certain employment sectors; for example, the organisation rates in government service, utilities, transport, and finance were all over 50 per cent in 1982, whilst that in manufacturing was over 35 per cent in the same year. The union movement's presence in these locations both provides it with a potential degree of strategic leverage that is far greater than the overall organisation rate might suggest would be possible and presents it with a huge challenge, since these are precisely the locations from whence women and the other victims of discrimination have been most assiduously excluded by capital.

CONCLUSION

In this chapter the question as to why the law entered industrial relations in postwar Japan has been answered by referring to the Occupation authorities' hope that the promulgation of a system of labour rights would help to democratise industrial relations and the wider society. The additional question as to the nature of the circumstances under which this occurred has been answered by emphasising the social–structural continuities between pre- and postwar Japan. These continuities, it was suggested, have existed in some tension with and, especially since the early 1970s, have tended to subvert the democratic impulse which originated with the Occupation. Thanks largely to the economic success with which they have been associated, these continuities have allowed the Japanese tradition to be 'reinvented' (cf. Hobsbawm 1984) once again, this time in the form of the largely secular and strikingly sociologised *Kigyôshugi*.

In the two chapters which follow I will be concerned to demonstrate two things: first, that the statutes upon which the postwar labour law system was based may be read as representing an instance of the continuities between pre- and postwar Japan; and second, that the reason why labour law has latterly become at least as much of a hindrance as a help to trade unions is because it has proved to be highly susceptible to *Kigyôshugi*-inspired readings on the part of the judiciary. The result of the latter is that it has reduced still further labour law's anyway limited capacity (see p. 15) to serve as a means for the enforcement of a certain democratism in the workplace. This will enable me to specify the concrete nature of *Kigyôshugi* in a particular sphere and, because of the very one-sided results of its presence, it will prepare the way for the final chapter in which the empirical dubiousness of *Kigyôshugi* accounts of the consensual nature of Japanese industrial relations will be indicated.

NOTE

1 The remainder of this section is a revised version of a part of Woodiwiss 1990c.

4

REFORM AND CONTINUITY IN LABOUR LAW

As a prelude to asking how it was that the leading cases of the postwar period were decided in the way they were and so also to attempting to judge the degree to which democratism was in fact embedded in labour law and could serve therefore as a factor inhibiting the development of any such discourse as *Kigyôshugi*, it is necessary to examine the general trajectory of legal development in the postwar period. In Chapter 2 it was argued that the Meiji legal system failed to sustain itself in the face of the absolutism bespoken by the militarist variant of *tennosei*. It was further argued that this was for reasons internal to the law as well external to it; that is, because the autonomy of the judiciary was severely restricted; because sanctions exercisable upon the judiciary's own behalf were absent; because means of redress on the part of the citizenry in relation to the state were also absent; because individual rights were anyway often subordinated to those of the head of the *ie*, as indicated by the structuring of the all-important registers (*Koseki*) on an *ie* basis; because the coexistence of patriarchal statism and private property made juridical consistency impossible to achieve and so undermined the independent authority of legal discourse; and, finally, as well as most significantly, because the law was negatively evaluated as compared to conciliation within *tennosei*.

LAW IN POSTWAR JAPAN

As was similarly made clear at the beginning of Part II, when the New Constitution was discussed, great efforts were made by the Occupation authorities and their Japanese allies (Oppler 1976) to correct at least some of these internal weaknesses. Individual

97

rights in general were greatly strengthened, with the ostensible exception of those of private property-holders. In addition, individuals acquired rights of redress against the state through administrative courts. The autonomy of the judiciary was considerably enhanced thanks to the Supreme Court's gaining of the power, if requested by the citizenry, to review government actions and legislation with a view to establishing their constitutionality. The judiciary's position was also strengthened by its gaining of the power to impose the sanctions of criminal law on its own behalf, although this power remains very underdeveloped as compared to that available in common law societies (Haley 1982a). Finally, as if to symbolise the potential significance of both these and the accompanying extra-legal developments, the registers were restructured on the basis of the nuclear rather than the extended family.

By depriving the *ie*, both institutionally and ideologically, of its critical role as the intermediary institution between the individual and the state, the restructuring of the registers struck at the patriarchal heart of *tennosei*. This was an attack continued by the two-stage reform of the Civil Code which occurred in 1947 and 1948, and whose principal concern was the reform of family relationships. As a result of the changes to the Code, primogeniture was abolished, wives gained control over their own property, mothers gained equality with fathers with respect to matters concerning children, women gained the same divorce rights as men and in numerous other ways the bases were created for a more egalitarian family structure and, by extension, a more individualised citizenry.

To create a basis for something does not, of course, ensure that the desired state of affairs will come about. Certainly, neither the democratisation of the Japanese family nor that of the relations between men and women more generally followed automatically from the introduction of these reforms. The same may be said of social relations more generally. As has already been mentioned, individual rights are still subject to a 'public welfare' test, which has meant that because of the invention of new duties they are more restricted than they need be. However, it should also be said that the general trend in decisions involving this test has been one of liberalisation (Beer 1984: ch. 12; in addition, see the cases reported in Itoh and Beer 1978: ch. 10 and Maki 1964: 3–155). This said, in the context of the argument that is presently being set forth, it is particularly important to point out, following Beer (1968), that the manner in which this has been achieved has typically been by 'harmonising' (i.e. hierarchising) conflicting positions rather than by balancing them. The judiciary is still very loath to exercise its powers of review and redress in relation to the acts and activities of the state (Haley 1986). However, this is not necessarily a bad thing in a democracy, where the governing party may be reasonably presumed to have a mandate from a majority of the population. Here again, for good or ill, the evidence suggests that this inhibition is somewhat less marked than it was, especially in the lower courts (Ishimine 1974). Strikingly, however, the meagre liberalisation, which, thanks to the effect of the public welfare test, occurred with respect to the legal rights of trade unions during the 1960s, was sharply reversed under the same dispensation during the 1970s when the duties of trade unions were re-emphasised.

As in most advanced capitalist societies, the public interest test has gained a general pertinence to the degree that it provides the basis for adjudication in the absence of clear guidance from statutes and codes and/or case law. Indeed in civil law countries its prominence in this role may sometimes be particularly marked, since judges and justices are less constrained by the *stare decisis* rule. As in other societies, the prominence of a public interest test carries the possibility that, in the absence of a clear, countervailing principle such as might be represented by the privileging of the rights of labour or of private property, judgements will depend upon the nature of the prevailing values and/or individual judges' understandings of them, as seems to be recognised to varying degrees by Japanese jurists (Itoh 1970: 785–804). What seems not to have been recognised by them, however, is that this possibility might also carry dangers, especially when the harmonising of rights is preferred to their balancing. In a society where the state continues to possess a still unrivalled social pre-eminence, the degree of danger depends very much upon the degree of pluralism that these values exhibit and/or that judges are prepared to recognise in relation to the rights of citizens, as well as upon the maintenance of democratic accountability. A point whose importance should be well understood in Japan, given the prewar experience of the 'judicial fascism' associated with the so-called 'free law' theory of Makino and his followers (Itoh 1970: 781–2).

In some contrast to the position adopted by scholars regarding its prewar status (see p. 54), several students of postwar Japanese law have been critical of the constraints imposed upon property right (e.g. Ukai and Nathanson 1968). Not only were such originally feudal forms of land-holding such as *emphyteusis* allowed to continue, but property rights, unlike 'life and liberty', were denied an American-style direct mention in Article 31, the 'due process' clause of the New Constitution. The fear, therefore, remains that the invocation of the public welfare test might yet prove to be particularly deleterious to the rights of property-holders. This seems to me to be an exaggerated fear: first, because under democratic conditions and therefore in contrast to the conditions obtaining in the prewar period, there is not the same danger that the public interest will be directly identified with that of the state; second, because as a matter of values and of fact the public welfare has been deemed in both the political and legal realms to include the protection and even the privileging of the rights of private property-holders.

Even before the LDP had established its political dominance, this privilege was apparent in the law. The case in which it became explicit was the so-called 'production control case' of *Japan* v. *Okada* (1950) in which the Supreme Court ruled that the production control strikes (*seisan kanri*), which had been such an outstanding feature of early postwar industrial relations, were unconstitutional. This pivotally important case will be discussed further below (see pp. 119–21). For the present it is sufficient to note that it very definitely privileged the rights of capital relative to those of labour and hence that there has been at the heart of postwar legal discourse a limit to the possible changes which might be wrought within that discourse so far as industrial relations are concerned. This is the limit which defines the Japanese legal system as capitalist and which thereby defines the contract of employment as an inherently unequal one, regardless of the freedoms and opportunities additionally granted to labour.

It is also a limit which in no sense has been weakened by Japanese contract law's lax requirements in relation to the establishment of whether or not a modification of contractual terms is allowable and/or has occurred, and which might otherwise seem to allow a smoother transition between *de facto* and *de jure* changes than in other societies (Sawada 1968, *passim* but especially: 95–7). I have insisted upon this point here, because, as was indicated above (p. 90), there are those who, under the often unacknowledged influence of *Kigyôshugi* and in particular of a belief in the intrinsic cooperativeness of *ie* and *mura*-type institutions, have recently begun to argue, like western 'human resources' ideologues, that such institutions are ones where the inequality as well as the antagonism between labour and capital has been overcome. This argument has been made despite the fact that any modification, actual, implied or imagined, to the employment contracts concerned has always stopped far short of any alteration to its basic assymmetry; i.e. it has always stopped far short of allowing labour anything other than a trivial share in the ownership and control of property in the means of production.

LABOUR LAW IN POSTWAR JAPAN

Although it has seldom been fully acknowledged in the pertinent literature, the same ambiguity as to what it might signify characterises the Trade Union Law as characterises the New Constitution. On the one hand, the passage of the law undoubtedly granted labour in both the private and public sectors rights and a degree of social recognition which it had never possessed before (only the police, firefighters and prison staff were excluded from this dispensation). On the other hand, it did so on the basis of a bill which had first been prepared by the Home Ministry's Social Bureau in 1925 (Garon 1987: 235 ff.) and under conditions where unionisation was anyway proceeding rapidly. The constraining and patriarchalist discourse that informed the unamended law was readily apparent to Leonard Appel of SCAP's Labour Advisory Committee (LAC), who, in Gould's paraphrase, noted the following:

> The Trade Union Law failed to 'fully and properly implement' a policy that would require an employer to adopt a 'strict hands-off policy' on the question of self-organization of his workers and to accept 'in good faith' the collective bargaining process. The L.A.C. also stated that the law provided no opportunity for a full and fair hearing for all parties concerned, and that the only procedure mentioned was '...criminal type sanctions'. The L.A.C.'s

statement that [the] 'majority rule principle is essential to effective collective bargaining' was to be echoed continuously during the Occupation.... Finally, the L.A.C. voiced its concern over the establishment of government supervision and controls over trade unions on the part of so-called administrative authorities and the consequent creation of a bureaucracy that might meddle in internal union affairs without any specific justification for this approach either at the time or in the future.

(Gould 1984: 27–8)

Also passed into law during the early days of the Occupation were two other labour laws which, although this has been commented upon even less often, similarly owed much to prewar state patriarchalism, the Labour Relations Adjustment Act (1946) and the Labour Standards Act (1947). However, before these laws and the amended Trade Union Law of 1949 are outlined in more detail, something more should be said about the constitutional provisions which pertain to labour. These provisions are the following:

Article 25. All people shall have the right to maintain the minimum standards of wholesome and cultured living.
In all spheres of life, the State shall use its best endeavors for the promotion and extension of social welfare and security, and of public health.
Article 27. All people should have the right and obligation to work.
Standards for wages, hours, rest and other working conditions shall be fixed by law.
Article 28. The right of workers to organise and to bargain and act collectively is guaranteed.

That these provisions should be susceptible to qualification by the same patriarchalism as the labour laws is a consequence of the fact that the Constitution in general remains marked by patriarchalism. That some at least of the socialist members of the *Diet* recognised these limitations and the dangers implicit in them is apparent from Quigley and Turner's (1956: 138) paraphrase of the House of Representatives discussion of the Constitution. The more and more unambiguous consequences of these ambiguous provisions on the ways in which the equally ambiguous labour laws have been read by the judiciary will be specified in the following chapter when the pertinent case law is discussed. First, however, the legislation of the Occupation period must be outlined more fully in order to establish the case for a reading of its basic structure as patriarchalist.

The Trade Union Law

The Trade Union Law was revised in 1949 in order to take account of the support which the Constitution had given to the most basic employee rights. However, it is still susceptible to a patriarchalist reading as I shall now demonstrate. Article 1 reads as follows:

> The purposes of the present law are to elevate the status of workers by promoting that they shall be on equal standing with their employer *in their bargaining with the employer*; to protect the exercise by workers of autonomous self-organization and association in trade unions *so that they may carry out collective action including the designation of representatives of their own choosing to negotiate the terms and conditions of work*; and to encourage the practice and procedure of collective bargaining *resulting in collective agreements governing relations between employers and workers* (emphases added).

As the italicised sections make very clear, no right is granted by the Law which is not immediately qualified by a statement as to the purpose for which it is granted – in no way should the grant of a right to self-organisation be understood as also warranting the choice of self-chosen ends. The Article reads as if those who drafted it were fearful lest the provision of even a few commas and/or full stops separating the clauses promulgating rights from those defining their proper purposes should give labour too much. Whether or not the drafters were aware of this possibility, the manner in which the Article is punctuated let alone written makes it very difficult for it to be read in such a way that employee rights may be said to be in any way separable from or privileged relative to the goal of establishing an orderly system of industrial relations and all of the duties this implies. Thus the

103

Law may be read as seeking to constrain even more the anyway not unconstrained Constitutional rights of employees by associating their granting with a definite and pre-defined ends. These ends very definitely did not include the allowance of what Marshall (1962: 116) termed 'a sort of secondary industrial citizenship' whereby trade union civil rights could be used for the purpose of asserting or enforcing political and social rights against the calls of duty.

Because labour's rights are defined in very general terms in the Constitution, the Trade Union Law contains none of the extensive exclusions to be found in the equivalent American legislation, such as those which relate to domestic, agricultural and government employees. For this and other reasons the revised Law has usually been compared favourably, from the trade union point of view, with the contemporaneously revised American National Labour Relations Act (NLRA), which was thenceforth most often known as the Taft–Hartley Act. However, three differences between the opening sections of the two laws should give one cause to doubt such judgements. The first is that the drafters of the American statute were not so fearful of punctuation or, more seriously, not so concerned to guard against rights being specified separately from purposes and the duties they imply. The second is that although the statements giving the reasons for the two laws are both set out in preambles, which are not legally binding and thus leave the determination of 'legislative intent' open to subsequent challenge, argument and alteration, this openness was largely illusory in the Japanese case. The judiciary's unsurprising reluctance to exercise its power of judicial review and the LDP's deference to the bureaucracy meant that the determination of the extent of labour's new rights as well as their enforcement was left very much in the hands of the bureaucracy and the conciliation- rather than rights-minded Labour Commissions established by the Act.

As it happens and at the margins, the consequences of this were not entirely detrimental to the labour interest. Indeed, it is clear to the present author that, weak as Japanese trade unions and especially minority ones currently are, they would be even weaker if they lost the modicum of protection afforded them by their status as what might be termed 'wards of the state'. The present concern is simply to correct the widespread view that the Trade Union Law, was, in the current American sense, a more liberal statute than the Taft–Hartley Act.

The third and final difference between the opening sections of the two statutes, which should cause one to question received opinion, is again one which emerges from reading the opening section of the Trade Union Law in its wider Japanese context and in particular in that of the fear of communism which gripped the government and the Occupation authorities in the late 1940s. This difference is one which implicitly reinforces the order-bringing 'intent' which I read as present in the Law, since it concerns a difference of textual emphasis as regards who were to be the primary recipients of the rights granted. In both cases, formally, the prime recipients of such rights were individual employees who wished to engage in collective action. However, whilst in the American case this primacy is referred to throughout the text (Woodiwiss 1990a: 238 ff.), in the Japanese case it is not stressed after the first clause of Article 1. This has the result that it often appears as if the unions are the prime recipients of the rights granted by the Japanese law. Thus, in clause 2 of Article 1, it is specifically 'trade unions' rather than, as in the American case, simply 'labor organisations' which are excused criminal liability when engaging in 'appropriate' acts, provided only that violence is not involved. Again, in Article 2, it is specifically 'trade unions' who only lose the Law's protection if they admit supervisors with authority in the personnel area or if they are in receipt of financial support from employers, whereas in the American case no supervisors may be members of the same labor organisations as those they supervise and employer financial support is designated an 'unfair labour practice' on the part of the employer, which should not necessarily affect the status of the union which admits them.

The point here is not so much that the substantive consequences of the divergent discursive strategies are great, although it is highly significant that the vast majority of Japanese supervisors belong to the same unions as those they supervise (see p. 151 and p. 161), as that it suggests that the discourse informing the Japanese text assumes that employee self-organisation can or should only take one form, that of a formally constituted trade union. These divergent discursive strategies as between the two statutes are also pertinent to the understanding of a further set of differences, namely why it is that Japanese labour law operates with a relatively tight definition of what constitutes a trade union and a relatively loose one of what constitutes an appropriate act – a pair of differences which has had disadvantageous as well as advantageous consequences for combinations of workers. One major disadvantage has been that the collective actions of unorganised workers are unprotected. On the other hand the primary advantage has been that, because, in contradistinction to the American case, there is no insistence upon representational exclusivity, it is relatively easy to form a minority or 'second' union, which thereafter is free to engage in a wide range of protected activity. However, the textual foregrounding of the term 'trade union' reinforces the suspicion voiced earlier that it is possible to read the intent of the Law as the containment of trade unionism. This is a reading whose plausibility is in my view further enhanced by the content of clause 4 of Article 1, which disqualifies as trade unions any organisations 'which principally aim at carrying on political or social movement [sic]'.

Chapter II of the Trade Union Law provides explicit confirmation of this reading. Although they are considerably less intrusive than the original provisions, the requirements as to what a union constitution should look like and as to how a union should carry on its affairs are remarkably specific. The NLRA originally contained no such requirements and even those added as part of the Taft–Hartley amendments are far less detailed. Interestingly, Article 5, perhaps reflecting SCAP's concern (see p. 101), requires unions to prove that they are autonomous, something which is assumed by the American legislation. It then goes on to require them to submit a constitution, which gives the union's name and address, and then insists on the following provisions: that there should be no discriminatory criteria for membership, that members should be treated equally and have participatory rights; that officials should be elected by secret ballot; that a general meeting should be held at least once a year; that a professionally audited financial report should be published every year; that strike votes should take the form of a secret ballot; and that constitutional changes require a majority vote, again in a secret ballot.

There is nothing inherently objectionable about any of these requirements and indeed the insistence that all important votes should take the form of secret ballots was probably essential if unions were to be able to maintain their autonomy of action relative to employers. However, the sheer number and specificity of the requirements makes it clear that the unions envisaged by the Law were, literally, a world away from the self-defined and therefore very varied associations known to the laws of England and the United States. By contrast, Japanese labour organisations were to be formed in a single mould chosen for them by the government's bureaucratic advisers. In this way the Law may be read as promising to simplify and order, even if it could not be expected immediately to pacify, the chaotic industrial world which so worried the employers and the authorities in the mid to late 1940s.

That the Law may be read as contributing to an ordering and not simply a democratising process is a reading that is also supported by the presence of the rather surprising proviso in the specification of the first of the 'unfair labour practices' prohibited by the Law. According to the first clause of Article 7, employers were forbidden from discharging or discriminating against any employee on the grounds of their union affiliation or their participation in 'proper acts of a trade union':

> Provided, however, that this shall not prevent an employer from concluding a collective agreement with a trade union to require, as a condition of employment, that the workers must be members of a trade union if such a trade union represents a majority of the workers in the particular plant or workplace in which such workers are employed.

In other words, like the American legislation, the Law appears to grant that there may be value in the post-entry closed shop, since not only may employees be disciplined for not joining up but also such a closed-shop is specifically protected against one possible route to its prohibition. The surprise lies in the unqualified nature of the protection offered by the Law, that is in the fact that the clause does not include the further proviso contained within the American legislation to the effect that termination of membership could not be for any reason other than 'failure...to tender the periodic dues and the initiation fees uniformly required'. In sum, either employer/union collusion against the interests of an individual employee was not thought possible or the latter's interests were not thought worthy of protection against the possibility of such an eventuality. All of which makes it especially significant that the 'duty to bargain' imposed by the second of the 'unfair labour practices' clauses is substantially less imperative than that imposed by the Taft–Hartley Act, thanks to the allowance made within it for the possibility that there may be 'fair and appropriate reasons' for a refusal to bargain.

As it turned out, despite the very general nature of the Law's definition of the category 'worker' ('those who live on their wages, salaries or other remuneration assimilable thereto'), the ways in which the first two unfair labour practice clauses were formulated facilitated the segmentation of the labour force with the result that a distinctively Japanese sub-class of labourers, so-called 'temporary workers', was created, which although they are continuously re-engaged nevertheless *de facto* if not necessarily *de jure* possess few of the rights of regular workers, not even, critically, the right to join an enterprise union. (It should be noted, however, that unions may choose to represent such workers, but that until recently they have typically chosen not to – in 1983 only 4.8 per cent of unions admitted temporary workers [Ohta 1988: 639].)

There are no significant differences between the two pieces of legislation concerning the remaining 'unfair labour practices' clauses – those which prohibit employer interference and discrimination against employees who file complaints under the provisions of the two Acts. This suggests that what otherwise might appear to be the rather slight differences between the wordings used in specifying the first two unfair labour practices were carefully considered. Taken together and contrasted to the American legislation from whence they were drawn, the first two Japanese clauses suggest rather clearly that it is possible to read the prime 'hope' of the Law as that unions should discipline a privileged core group of employees whilst not themselves offering too great a challenge to employers.

The remaining Articles of Chapter II grant unions engaged in 'proper acts' immunity from civil suits for damages, provide for changes in the use of union funds, specify the procedure to be followed when dissolution is desired, and grant unions legal personality.

Chapter III affords another significant contrast to the Taft–Hartley Act, since, as if to re-emphasise what I have suggested was the imagined hope of the drafters, it is solely concerned with something which only warrants a sub-clause in the American law, namely the collective agreement. This should be a written, signed or sealed document of not more than three years validity, which in the event of its being applied to more than three-quarters of the labour force in a particular workplace should be extended to all of the 'regular' labour force. Interestingly and presumably in order to discourage labour mobility, according to Article 18:

> When a majority part of the workers of a similar kind in a certain locality come under application of one collective agreement, the Minister of Labour or the prefectural governor may, at the request of either one or both of the parties concerned...and according to the resolution of the Labour Relations Commission, take the decisions [*sic*] to extend the compulsory application of the collective agreement... to all remaining workers of the same kind employed in the same locality and their employers.

> In case the Labour Relations Commission deems...that the collective agreement in question contains inappropriate [i.e. improper] provisions, the Commission may amend those provisions

In this passage, then, the overall state-managerialist intent of the Law is finally made explicit.

The final two chapters of the Law concern the aforementioned Labour Relations Commissions and the penalties to be imposed upon those who contravene the rules laid down by the Law. Of these two chapters, only the first will be discussed here. The Commissions comprise a central and a subordinate set of prefectural bodies, upon which employers, employees and 'the public interest' are represented equally (the public members should not include a majority of any one political party). They possess the 'authority to perform conciliation, mediation and arbitration of labour disputes', as well as the power to receive, investigate and adjudicate upon complaints relating to unfair labour practices. Where either party to a complaint requests a review of a prefectural commission's adjudication, this may be heard, at the petitioner's discretion, either by the Central Labour Relations Commission or by the appropriate District Court.

The Labour Relations Adjustment Law

The traditional fear of labour and unions as potentially disruptive and the concern that the New Constitution might have given too much to labour, both of which remained largely implicit even in the amended Trade Union Law, may be read as having become explicit in the Labour Relations Adjustment Law (LRAL) of 1946. As is clear from the imperative language of the first five Articles of the Law, labour is expected to exercise its rights under the Trade Union Law only as a very last resort and only *after* it has requested the help of state agencies in the form of the Labour Commissions:

Article 1. The aim of this Law shall be...to promote a fair adjustment of labour relations and to prevent or settle labour disputes and thereby to contribute to the maintenance of industrial peace and to economic development.

Article 2. The parties concerned with labour relations shall make special endeavours mutually to promote proper and fair labour relations, and to fix by collective agreement matters concerning the establishment as well as management of regular agencies to adjust differences constantly, and, in the event of labour disputes occurring, to settle them autonomously in all sincerity.

Article 3. The Government shall assist the parties concerned with labour relations in order thereby to prevent to the utmost the occurrence of acts of dispute.

Article 4. Nothing in this Law shall be construed either to prevent the parties from determining for themselves their labour relations or from adjusting the differences of their claims concerning labour relations by direct negotiations or collective bargaining or to relieve the parties concerned with labour relations of their responsibility for making such endeavours.

Article 5. In affecting any adjustment under this present Law, the parties and the Labour Relations Commission and other organs concerned shall as far as possible utilise every appropriate convenience to expedite the disposal of the case.

Although the Law provides for the appointment of 'special

110

members for adjustment', by insisting on the propriety of resort to conciliation, etc. as well as by charging the Labour Commissions rather than a separate institution like the United States' Federal Mediation and Conciliation Service with these tasks, it was also made clear that the Commissions were to exercise their adjudicatory function only very sparingly and therefore that those who drafted the Law saw little in either the employment relation or the law relating to it that might give rise to issues of principle. As conceptualised in the law, the employment relation in Japan remains very much a status relation rather than a contractual one. The statuses of the parties have been equalised to a degree, but the possibility that they might be further and variably equalised as a result of private agreements between the parties concerned was not anticipated and certainly not encouraged. In sum, the Law may be read as providing more of a vehicle for the expression of the state's preferences than a state-provided and supported mechanism for the establishment and protection of changing private preferences.

In Articles 6 and 7 a very broad and, when viewed comparatively, a generous definition of the 'acts of dispute' of interest to and ostensibly now protected by the law is provided:

> an act of dispute shall mean a strike, a slowdown, a lockout and other acts and counter acts, hampering the normal course of work of an enterprise, performed by the parties concerned with labour relations with the object to [sic] attaining their respective claims.

The Articles that follow immediately suggest that the thinking behind this apparent generosity may have been somewhat disingenuous, since they are concerned to define certain industries and services (transport, the post office, telecommunications, water, gas, electricity, private and public health care and any others the Prime Minister shall so designate) as utilities, all of which later become subject to 'emergency adjustment' as specified in Articles 35–2 to 35–5. According to these Articles, if 'an act of dispute gravely imperil the normal operation of the national economy', then the Prime Minister shall, after consulting the Labour Commission, order the Commission to intervene even if mediation, which normally requires the consent of at least one of the parties, is the mode of adjustment ordered and

111

without any possibility of appeal or review – shades of 'sabre mediation' (see p. 65).

Perhaps the clearest confirmation that the thrust of this whole body of legislation may be read as the desirability of the exclusion of a discourse of rights from industrial relations and the maintenance of a special role for the state and its agencies, is the fact that the preferred modes of adjustment are the same as they were in the prewar period, namely conciliation (*chotei*), mediation (*assen*) and arbitration, in that order. Of these, the first is potentially the most intrusive since, although typically it is expected to be, and generally is, requested by one or other of the parties directly concerned it may be that, according to Article 12, that 'on his own initiative, the Chairman of the competent Labour Relations Commission shall appoint a conciliator from the panel'. (According to Sugeno [nd.: 40] only 3 per cent of conciliations were initiated by the Commissions in 1983.)

All in all, although it is often said that Japanese labour law is uniquely favourable to labour in that it specifies no 'unfair labour practices' on the labour side to balance those that constrain employers, it seems to me that the existence of the Labour Relations Adjustment Law renders any such provisions largely redundant since, because of it, few disputes reach the point at which secondary actions, for example, could be mounted let alone have a bearing on the outcome. This said, the courts have had no difficulty discovering the appropriate prohibitions when called upon to do so (see p. 137).

The Labour Standards Law

Perhaps surprisingly, although in its coverage it is far more extensive than its equivalents in Britain and the United States, the last of the initial trio of labour laws, namely the Labour Standards Law of 1947, is the one least suggestive of the distinctively patriarchalist cast that is here claimed to distinguish Japanese labour law. All such laws and their associated common law rules connote a certain paternalism, as British and American feminist critics of the provisions relating to 'protective' restrictions on women's employment have emphasised. Moreover, the unusually broad and detailed coverage of the Japanese statute is the result of simple necessity in a situation where, thanks to its almost complete absence in the prewar period, individual labour law had to be created virtually *de novo* after the war. It is for this reason that the Labour Standards Law is such a compendious piece of legislation, covering as it does the labour contract, rules governing wages, holidays, women and juvenile workers, training, accident compensation, disciplinary codes and dormitory regulations. Many of these provisions were either established in common law or legislated for separately in other jurisdictions.

The Public Corporation and National Enterprise Labour Relations Law

What will be referred to hereafter as the Public Corporations Labour Law (PCLL) was passed in December 1948 and may be read as exemplifying the increasing agreement between the Occupation authorities and non-socialist cabinets that the threat represented by the left had to be taken seriously and pre-emptive measures taken wherever possible (Harari 1973: 59 ff.). Because this law was strenuously opposed by socialist cabinet members and some civil servants, it is usually argued that it was largely the handiwork of SCAP. However, as against this position I wish to suggest that the text contains more than enough evidence to suggest that it was actually of a piece with the rest of the body of legislation currently under review. In line with the patriarchalism which I have argued informs all of the legislation, this Law opens by declaring parenthetically that its object of concern is the 'responsibility of participants in labour relations procedures' (emphasis added). In Articles 1 and 2, a special responsibility is placed upon public corporation employees in the railway, salt and tobacco industries. This special responsibility is that of 'securing the uninterrupted operation' of the aforementioned industries and services and its necessity is explained as being the result of their central importance to 'the public welfare'.

The possibility that trade unions might in some way represent interests antithetical to the public welfare is suggested in a rather oblique way by the casual introduction of a new employee right in the course of what otherwise appears to be the straightforward reiteration of basic employee rights represented by Article 4. This new right is the right 'to refrain from organising trade unions'. Although this phrasing immediately calls to mind Section 7 of the THA, in the light of all that has been said above, and especially in the light of the lack of concern for the plight of temporary workers (see p. 108), it seems extremely unlikely that the introduction of this new right was inspired by the same concern to absolutise individual freedom as was the case in the American law. Rather, as is suggested by the very fact of its inclusion in a special law relating to state-owned enterprises rather than in the Trade Union Law itself, it seems more reasonable to read the new right as originating in a concern to ensure that employees of such enterprises should be as free as possible to serve whatever the state defines as the public welfare.

What this law may be read as making very clear, then, is how quickly the reluctant character of the state's recognition of trade unions made itself felt, especially in areas which were directly within its purview. Thus, in striking contrast to the situation at the same time in Britain where trade unions were encouraged to believe that, because of their involvement, the newly nationalised industries would be better able to serve the public interest, the PCLL may be read as seeking to ensure that unions had as little say as possible in the equivalent industries. If, because of the Constitution, the employees of state-owned enterprises had to be allowed to join unions, should they insist upon it, the Law provides the means whereby the threat perceived to be represented by trade unions may be reduced. In Article 8, and this was another new feature in labour law, 'matters pertaining to... management and operation' are specifically excluded from collective bargaining. Moreover, Article 17 stated that:

> Employees and unions shall not engage in a strike, a slow-down or any other act of dispute hampering the normal course of operation...nor shall any employees as well as union members and union officers conspire to effect, instigate, or incite to, such prohibited conduct.

The only recourse available to public sector unions in the event of a breakdown of negotiations is to their own specially constituted Labour Commission. As severe and as rigorously enforced as these restrictions are (Sugeno 1979: 9), they are not as indicative of the depth of the antagonism between the state's discourse about itself and trade unionism as the requirement that only serving employees can be union officers in the public sector, which was part of the Law when it was first passed. This requirement was imposed by Article 4(3) and it may be read as making manifest the state's insistence that wherever possible it should retain the disciplinary upper hand – in the latter half of the 1950s the state repeatedly sacked union leaders for engaging in illegal acts of dispute and then used their lack of employee status as a pretext for suspending collective bargaining (see pp. 123–9).

However, it was not sufficient that unions should be denied any means of enforcing their claims, or even talking about resorting to them. Thus those contaminated by their handling of a trade union virus whose most common symptom was thought to be insubordination, had to be, in a certain sense, isolated from the enterprise for fear that they might corrupt it. This was the effect of the seldom commented upon Article 7, which makes it necessary for those wishing to take up full-time union positions in a particular enterprise both to be employees of the enterprise concerned and to gain the permission of their employers and which, tellingly, reads as follows:

> The employee who obtained [sic] the permission...shall be treated as a temporarily retired employee so long as the permission is valid, and shall not be paid any kind of remuneration.

This, in sum, was the law which may be read as having explicitly confirmed the patriarchalist nature of Japan's postwar labour legislation.

Given that civil servants were, in the words of Article 15 of the Constitution, 'servants of the whole community and not of any group thereof', it was not surprising that even more restrictions (a National Personnel Authority replaced the fledgling collective bargaining institutions) were more or less simultaneously imposed upon them in the form of revisions to the National Public Service Law and the Local Public Service Law, both of which thereafter contained equivalents to Article 17 of the PCLL. In 1952 the restrictions on public enterprise workers were also applied to the employees of Nippon Telephone and Telegraph Public Corporation (NTT), as well as to those employed in such as the postal, forestry and government broadcasting and printing services. In the same year they were applied to the employees of local public enterprises such as transportation undertakings and utilities of all kinds by the Local Public Enterprise Labour Law, which significantly was extended to cover the increasingly ideologically recalcitrant teachers in 1954. Finally, in 1953 these restrictions were extended to private industries in which the state claimed a special interest, namely the coal mining and the electricity generation and supply industries. In sum, although it must be acknowledged that SCAP ardently wished that Japanese civil servants should be deprived altogether of trade union rights, like their American equivalents, it nevertheless seems reasonable to suggest that in this as in other aspects of its labour policy, the Japanese state needed little prodding by SCAP to do what it did (cf. Garon 1987: 237 ff.). At any event, not only did the state gain a means of disciplining sections of the labour force that it deemed to be of special significance to itself, but it also reaped what I am sure was not the totally uncovenanted benefit of a union movement divided by, amongst other things, the exigencies which flow from having to face divergent legal circumstances.

CONCLUSION

It thus seems entirely appropriate to complete this reading of Japan's postwar legislation by pointing out the similarity between the patriarchal and highly ordered arrangements it envisioned and the 'limited pluralism' envisioned but only partially achieved by the reform bureaucrats of the 1920s and 1930s (see p. 45). In concluding this chapter it is, moreover, important to note that there was one particular instance of continuity as between the pre-and postwar legal systems which greatly reduced the likelihood that the law, irrespective of its ideological content, could serve for long as a source of resistance to a discourse such as *Kigyôshugi*. Although most of the internal reasons for the law's prewar weakness listed at the beginning of this chapter no longer held after it, one at least retained much of its potency. This was the ideological bias against any sort of legal proceedings and in favour of conciliation in its varying forms. Moreover, as was made clear in the discussion of the LRAL, this bias was embedded in the heart of the new labour law system. It is apparent from many general as well as more specialised texts on Japanese law (see, for example, Noda 1976; Sawada

1968; and many of the papers collected in Tanaka 1976 and Mehren 1963), that this preference has been uncritically carried over into postwar thinking about the law on the grounds that it is simply part of 'the Japanese way'. I say 'uncritically carried over', because the writers of such texts still never pose let alone address such questions as: Is it a freely chosen preference? and Who benefits from this preference?.

In other words, the ascription of non-litigiousness to the Japanese people is every bit as much a part of *Kigyôshugi* as it was a part of *tennosei*. Thus, in so far as the answers to these questions remain the same as they were when they were posed in relation to prewar society (see p. 58), the ideological articulation and enforcement of a preference for conciliation over resort to the law indicates the existence of a substantive extra-legal ideology that, as in all other advanced industrial societies (for the United States, see Woodiwiss 1990a: ch. 8), gained entry to the law via the notion of 'the public welfare'. The specifications of the effects of this ideology and of how they confirm the plausibility of the reading of the basic laws that has just been presented are the primary aim of the chapter which follows.

5

THE CASE LAW OF RELUCTANT RECOGNITION

Ideally, in a civil law system such as Japan's, case law and even the judgements of the Supreme Court should be of little consequence. In reality, of course, the proliferation of statutes and changing social conditions mean that divergent readings of the law become ever more likely and that authoritative readings become increasingly necessary. Postwar Japan has proved to be no exception to this rule, except that because of the poverty of the unions, the expensiveness of legal proceedings and the pre-emptive effects of *Kigyôshugi*, the courts have had far fewer opportunities to set out their readings than in comparable European legal systems.

Of these reasons for the relative paucity of Japan's case law, the last is by far the most important. Not only does the presence of *Kigyôshugi* in the discourses of production at Japanese workplaces dramatically reduce the likelihood of internal disputes becoming public in the first place, but because of its insistence on the preferability of conciliation, it also reduces the likelihood of them providing grist for the juridical mill. The result is that most of the disputes which have the potential to be legally interesting come before the Labour Commissions, who typically conciliate them and so deprive them of any legal significance as regards the specification of the rights and duties of the parties involved. Moreover, the courts too would appear to prefer that disputes are conciliated rather than decided, since they often encourage out-of-court settlements even in mid-trial. In the light of the way in which the law is pre-empted, avoided and thus, to a degree derogated, it should come as no surprise that, with a few minor and/or transitory exceptions, when it has been invoked labour law has contributed to the gradual establishment of *Kigyôshugi*'s hegemony within Japanese workplaces. This has been especially the case since the early 1970s. This said, a reading of the case law nevertheless provides plenty of evidence that Japanese workplaces are often, in fact, far less harmonious than they are commonly pictured to be, as well as some that suggest that it remains a possibility, albeit an extremely unlikely one, that labour law may yet be made to reinforce discourses other than *Kigyôshugi*.

CASE LAW I: CONSTITUTIONAL ISSUES

No sooner had the amendments to the Trade Union Law been passed than the Supreme Court was asked in the case of *Okada v. Japan* (1950) to consider the legality of a sit-down or 'production control' strike in which the strikers had not only continued production, but had also sold some of the products of their labour in order to meet their wage and other bills (Maki 1964: 273–81). For this the strike leaders were arrested, tried and found guilty of the theft of company property. The argument that the individual defence attorneys set out before the Court drew on some or all of the following points: (1) that production control was protected by the 'and other [activity]' clause in Article 7 of the Labour Relations Adjustment Law; (2) that the right to strike was constitutionally protected and therefore could not be restricted; (3) that production control represented an instance of strike activity and therefore shared in the protection granted by the Constitution; (4) that the lower court had accepted that production control was legal where owners artificially restricted production; and (5) that the strikers were therefore in legal possession of the factory and its contents.

The Court dismissed each of these arguments and confirmed the decisions of the lower courts. A consideration of the Court's reasoning provides an excellent context within which to gain a fuller appreciation of what Beer means when he says that Japanese jurists do not so much balance conflicting rights as 'harmonise' them (see p. 99). In the Court's opinion, while production control may indeed count as an instance of the 'other [activity]' envisaged in the Labour Relations Adjustment Law, this fact indicates nothing one way or another as to its legality. Concerning the defence's second point, the Court argued that labour's constitutional rights 'to organise, and to bargain and act collectively' did not stand alone but coexisted with 'fundamental human rights such as the right to equality, civil liberties, and the right to property'. It continued that:

> It is desirable to have harmony between these various general fundamental human rights and the rights of labor; not to disrupt this harmony is a limitation on the propriety of the right to strike. Where must this point of harmony be sought? It is determined by an overall examination of the spirit of the system of law. Of course, the liberties of the employer and his property rights are also not absolutely unlimited and it is natural that they be restricted to a certain extent for the benefit of labor's right of collective action and so forth. But...it must be recognised that to oppress the free will of the employer and to obstruct his control over his property are not permissible. Such action gives undue weight to the right of labour to strike, improperly infringes on the rights of the employer, and disrupts the harmony required by law.
>
> (Maki 1964: 175–6)

Manifestly, such reasoning does not so much harmonise the rights of labour with those of property as assume the subordination of the former to the latter. The rights of capital are considered to be more important than those of labour. They are accompanied by the adjective 'fundamental', they are dignified by the title 'human rights' and they are described as 'the mainstay' of the country's legal order. The harmony that is evoked is something predefined and taken for granted. It is a condition wherein an allowance has already been made for the rights of labour, an allowance that preserves 'the spirit of the system of law' and so preserves 'the free will of the employer'. It is therefore a harmony which would be disrupted if the right to strike were limitless.

This view was repeated in the course of the Court's rebuttal of the defence's third point. Production control, it argued, is not simply an instance of strike activity and therefore is not protected by the Constitution. This is because it exceeds the 'non-fulfillment of the obligation of the labor force to perform' that is instanced by a strike and shakes 'the foundations of the private property of the entrepreneur'. Labour does not 'naturally possess the rights of employment and of earnings from the enterprise and does not have authority in respect to the right of operation' (emphasis added). Rather these rights and this authority inhere in the capitalist, to whom 'both the profits and losses of an enterprise are traceable'. Thus, in the Court's view, production control is illegal even where no theft of company property has occurred. The Court's dismissal of the defence's fourth point was so summary that it added nothing to its argument, whilst its more elaborate discussion of the fifth point predictably concluded on the basis of its earlier reasoning that the union was not in legal possession of the factory and had been guilty of theft when it sold company property.

In sum, the postwar judicial history of Japan's labour law begins with what was for Japan an unparalleledly powerful assertion of capital's privileged position in society and, because of this, in the law too. The latter reasoning is also interesting in the light of the tension between it and the discourse of class-denial that is intrinsic to the sociologising of the *kokutai* outlined in Chapter 3 and which will be discussed further in Chapter 6. It therefore suggests, in line with the argument advanced in the previous chapter, that at least initially a rather different conception of the nature of Japanese enterprises informed labour law as compared to that which is propagated by *Kigyôshugi*. This was a conception that stressed the conflicting interests of capital and labour and which in a democratic context might therefore have been expected to lead the law to be concerned to protect both sets of interests equally.

Although the Court did not make the point explicitly, one of the principles upon which it based itself was one whose restrictive potential has already been mentioned (see p. 74), namely the rider added to Article 12 to the effect that 'the people...shall refrain from any abuse of these freedoms and rights and shall always be responsible for using them in the public welfare' (this article was, however, listed first amongst the Court's references). The relativising of the people's rights and freedoms was a theme that the Court returned to, this time explicitly, in its next significant labour law case, which will be referred to here as *The Tokyo Electric Express Railway Company Case* (1951) (Maki 1964: 285–8). This was a case that came before the Court in 1951 and related to circumstances where several employees of a railway company provided stories to Communist Party newspapers, which alleged corruption in the relations between the company and the union. The company invoked its disciplinary regulations and dismissed the authors of the stories for slandering the company and hindering its efficient operations. In response the dismissed workers sued for reinstatement on the grounds that their rights to freedom of expression, as well as their trade union rights, had been violated. The Court's dismissal of this argument centred on the free speech issue and largely concurred with the judgement of the lower court that:

> The act of publication carried out under article 21 [the free speech clause] *naturally* cannot be interpreted as having been guaranteed without any attendant responsibilities. Accordingly, persons who engage in such acts of publication must inevitably find themselves in a position in which they are responsible under both criminal and civil law for such acts.... When the conduct of the appellants...came under the disciplinary regulations of the said company, then a situation arose that *naturally* and necessarily had to be dealt with by the said company in accordance with the... regulations and it is impossible to construe Article 21 of the Constitution as having any effect on the validity of the above disciplinary regulations [emphasis added].

What is particularly interesting about this judgement, apart from its substantive content, is again the confident way in which the term 'naturally' is used, especially since it is used in the context of a judgement that sounds far from natural to liberal–democratic ears and perhaps especially to American ones. My suggestion is that what allowed this confidence was an unspoken, background assumption as to how things should be in a *Japanese* enterprise which corresponded to the patriarchal *ie* ideal. The latter, then, was able to enter legal discourse thanks to the Court's insistence that constitutional freedoms were not absolute and could be qualified either in the light of Court determined considerations of the public welfare or because of 'obligations freely contracted'. This case therefore represents the founding moment of *Kigyôshugi* as far as labour law is concerned – employee rights are not only subordinate to those of the employer but also do not enjoy the same status.

The possibility that individual institutions might become

laws unto themselves as far as the constitutional rights of individuals were concerned became even clearer during the course of the Court's judgement in the next important labour law case to come before it. This was the case which will be referred to here as *The Tokachi Girls' Commercial School Case* (Maki 1964: 283–92). This case came before the Court in 1952, just as the Occupation was ending. It involved a young woman teacher whose contract of employment stipulated that, whilst her membership of the Communist Party would not cause her to be dismissed, she should nevertheless refrain from engaging in political activity within school grounds. Soon after her employment commenced, the teacher concerned was alleged to have sold to her students copies of a book published by the Japan Young Communist League and entitled *The Problem of Love*. Largely for this reason she was sacked. Rather than accept her dismissal, she sued for the nullification of her contract on the basis that it violated her fundamental human rights. She was not successful and her quest for reinstatement was finally ended by the Supreme Court's declaration:

> That the fundamental human rights guaranteed by the Constitution are not absolute and can be limited by obligations freely contracted under special public or private law.

Throughout the 1950s, the various issues prompted by the restrictions on the rights of public sector employees bubbled beneath the surface as time and again they struck in defiance of these restrictions. Matters finally came to a head in 1957 when the National Railway Workers' Union (Kokuro) was chosen to spearhead that year's Spring Labour Offensive (*shunto*). Although agreement was reached quite quickly in the private sector, the struggle in the public sector became a long drawn out one. The government reneged on a conciliation agreement. Railway and other public service workers were dismissed and otherwise disciplined for taking part in strikes, including some who were union leaders. Finally, the management of the National Railways invoked section 4(3) of the PCLL (only employees may be union officers) and refused to bargain with Kokuro and any other rail unions whose leaderships still included the dismissed workers. The same scenario was replayed the following year, only this time it involved the Postal Workers' Union (Zentai) and it ended in the courts. It eventually reached the Supreme Court in 1966 as *Toyama et al.* v. *Japan* or *The Tokyo Central Post Office Case*. Throughout the eight years that the case progressed through the court system, it occupied a position close to the heart of Japanese politics (for a sampling of establishment views on union rights during this period see Maki 1980: 114–16). Also, thanks to the intervention of the ILO in connection with section 4(3)'s contravention of its convention concerning freedom of association, it became an object of some international interest. The pertinence of, and the complications caused by, these facts have already been explained in some detail by Harari (1973) and so need not be discussed here. Instead I will concentrate on setting out the grounds given by the Court for its judgement that Article 17 (prohibition of acts of dispute) of the PCLL was not unconstitutional as counsel for Zentai had argued. In the course of this account it should become apparent that it is not impossible that, provided the social balances are favourable, the freedom to make law that is allowed by the existence of a public interest test and a harmonising methodology may sometimes be exercised to the advantage of labour as well as to that of capital, although always within the limits defined by *Okada* v. *Japan* (1950).

The opinion of the Court's majority begins by repeating Article 28 of the Constitution and acknowledging that the PCLL curtails the rights granted by it. Under such circumstances, the majority continues,

> a legal interpretation of the substantive law curtailing fundamental rights... must be sound and reasonable...so as to maintain harmony and balance between these two groups of rights.
>
> (Itoh and Beer 1978: 90)

In this instance the majority found that 'the point of harmony' may be found by acknowledging that public employees are indeed employees like their colleagues in private industry and that they should therefore enjoy the same rights, except that sometimes the particular nature of their duties requires that there should be some restrictions upon them in 'the interests of the nation as a whole'. Moreover, any restrictions imposed in such circumstances should be minimal, related to the degree to which the duties concerned are 'imbued with a public interest', enforced by civil sanctions alone where possible and compensated for by the making of alternative arrangements for pay bargaining and the resolution of grievances. As a result of an examination of the historical emergence of the legislation concerned with public employees, the majority found that the legislation had in fact been informed by exactly these principles. Also, thanks to the Court's sudden readoption of a very English, close or 'black letter' approach to the reading of statutes, a particularly strong indication of the influence of these principles was to be found in the absence of any provision for criminal as opposed to civil sanctions in the PCLL where legitimate dispute activities were concerned. On this basis the convictions imposed on the postal workers were overturned and the case remanded to the lower court for further proceedings.

An immediate indicator that the reasoning just outlined is somewhat strained is the fact that four of the twelve justices dissented. However, an even stronger indication that the dissenting minority suspected that the majority were straining for a particular social effect, namely the quietening of a labour interest that was then very militant, is apparent in the latter's not unreasonable contention that the simple absence of any direct mention of criminal sanctions from the PCLL does not mean that they were inapplicable in cases where public employees were concerned. Moreover, the following passage makes it plain that in the opinion of the minority, any supposition of any legislative intent to the contrary on the part of the majority was simply a means of rationalising a decision that had been taken for other and more immediate reasons:

> the commissioners representing the government, at the time of the Diet discussion of the bill for the PELRL [PCLL], repeatedly explained their view that Article 1, paragraph 2 of the Labor Union Law would cease to be applicable to dispute activities engaged in by employees of public corporations as a result of enactment of Article 17 or the PELRL [PCLL].... After discussion, the bill was passed. So the intent of the legislature may be presumed to be the same as that of the commissioners. Due respect should be paid to such legislative intent.
>
> (Itoh and Beer 1978: 101)

In sum and in the light of the dissenters trenchant arguments, it may be suggested that the majority's tortured reasoning in this case indicated that it might have been mindful of a larger set of public interest considerations than it was prepared to make explicit. Perhaps it thought that the state's and perhaps even the nation's face could be saved by both preserving the constitutionality of, and also slightly softening (employees could still be sanctioned and even dismissed for engaging in acts of dispute) the impact of, the PCLL. The principle that appears most likely to have informed the majority's reasoning was made explicit by one of its members on the next occasion that the Court was asked for its opinion of the constitutionality of a labour law, this time the National Public Service Law, namely in *Japan* v. *Sakane et al.* or *The Court Worker Incitement Case* of 1969:

> When a literal interpretation of a provision of law leaves doubts about its constitutionality, insofar as possible we should apply to this provision a reasonable, qualified interpretation and construe it to be in harmony with the intent of the Constitution.
>
> (Itoh and Beer 1978: 117)

In other words and ironically, the Court's readoption of a 'black letter' approach allowed it to apply what was in fact a socially pragmatic methodology of law-finding instead of invoking a set of substantive principles (for similar developments in the United States, see Woodiwiss 1990a: ch. 8). Before illustrating in some detail the way in which this separation of the law from the principles that were formerly its anchors opened the way for ever more explicitly *Kigyôshugi* readings of what sort of behaviour is sanctioned by labour law, brief mention must be made of the fate of the PCLL's section 4(3) and its equivalents in the laws applied to civil servants proper. As a result of the complexity of the political quadrille that ensued once the ILO had become involved, it took nearly as long for a partial resolution of the problem to be achieved as it took *Tokyo Central Post Office* to progress through the courts. The government finally ratified the ILO's convention 87 and abrogated section 4(3) of the PCLL and its equivalents in 1965.

In the light of the argument that has just been outlined, it should come as no surprise to discover that, although a certain softening of sanctions was repeated in connection with civil servants (Beer 1984: 234–5), these trade union victories did not presage a permanent turnaround in the legal fortunes of public sector unions more generally. For a while the trend of judicial decisions in 'acts of dispute' cases quite markedly favoured the unions (Sugeno 1979: 34–5, n.63). However, this trend was of no help to the civil service unions involved in the aforementioned *Court Worker Incitement Case*, in the course of which Justice Irokawa produced an argument in favour of the constitutionality of politically inspired acts of dispute that was as ingenious as, and far more strongly supported than, that produced by the majority in *Tokyo Central Post Office* (Itoh and Beer 1978: 121–30). Something of the reviving assertiveness of the Court's patriarchalism is communicated by the tone of the following extract from the passage in which the Court majority prepared to dismiss Irokawa's argument and give vent to the affront that it felt its own dignity had suffered because some court employees had publicly sought to express views critical of the government:

> With respect to restriction of the dispute activities of court employees, in the light of the facts that the whole judicial power is vested in the courts, and that the courts have the mission, based on this inherent state power, to protect the rights and liberties of the people and to maintain the social order of the state, the staff functions of those engaged in such judicial duties carried out by the courts are generally of a strongly public nature. We must say it is likely that an interruption of those functions will obstruct the achievement of that mission and, in turn, will seriously impair the daily life of the nation.
>
> (Itoh and Beer 1978: 108–9)

By 1973 this tone had been transformed into a positively anti-union tone as regards the public sector. The softening of sanctions that had ensued after *Tokyo Central Post Office* was reversed in *Tsuruzono* v. *Japan* (1976), which related to a two-hour strike by some civil servants in 1958 against the proposed revisions to the Police Duties Law. The legal basis upon which what was to a significant degree a new Court (between 1970 and

1972 seven of the fifteen justices were replaced by more conservative appointees, some of whom had no legal training whatsoever) made its decision was, in Beer's paraphrase, as follows:

> the view that illegal dispute activities by public employees and the laws can be given a 'so-called constitutional qualified interpretation' is itself contrary to proper legal procedure under Article 31 [of the Constitution]. Neither can such dispute activities be divided according to legal and illegal acts, greater or lesser illegality, incitement and acts ordinarily attendant to disputes, or acts meriting or not meriting criminal punishment depending on varying degrees and kinds of illegality.
>
> (Beer 1984: 235–6)

Interestingly, this reversal of precedent was marked by a shift in the way the general welfare was spoken of – from the less abstract 'peoples' daily lives' of the more liberal decisions to the much vaguer 'common interest of the people' of *Tsuruzono* v. *Japan*. This is a shift which makes it much harder to talk of degrees of injury to the general welfare and hence of degrees of illegality, as well as one which has been maintained in later Supreme Court decisions.

The undeclared social, but equally determinant (no doubt as to the constitutionality of the public sector union laws was entertained), grounds upon which the judgement was made appear to have had a lot to do with the still further increased militancy of the public sector employees. Many in conservative circles preferred to think of this militancy as a simple consequence of the liberalising of the law (the mistaken relaxing of patriarchal authority) rather than as a consequence of a set of very complex and fraught industrial relations problems to which both sides had made a contribution (Sugeno 1979: 14–15). The reversal and carelessness of precedent involved in *Tsuruzono* was repeated in relation to local civil servants in *Japan* v. *Ogawa et al.* (1976) and in relation to the PCLL in *Japan* v. *Kikuchi* (1977), where part of the Court's reasoning was even supported by a favourable reference to the notorious and long abrogated Peace Preservation Act. In addition, the distaste for political action of any kind on the part of civil servants was reiterated in *Japan* v. *Osawa* (1974) and in *The Teachers' Union President Case* (1980, see Beer 1984: 239). In the last of these a union president and a colleague were sentenced to a year in prison for leading a 'political strike' for higher wages and the right to strike in 1974 (Beer 1984: 236–8). Even union activity as such would now appear to be frowned upon in the public sector with the Supreme Court's 1982 upholding of the administrative order to take down a union notice board at issue in *Japan* v. *Kikuchi* (1977).

All that said, it is important to record that, most likely, it was largely because of the rather different political–economic conditions that obtained during much of the 1980s (export difficulties, the revival of the LDP and the privatisation of the key public corporations) rather than because of the disciplinary effectivity of the law that there was a significant reduction in public sector union militancy. Moreover, the legal issue still remains a live one, albeit for a far smaller number of public employees after the privatisations of the 1980s. This is because, thanks to the pertinence of wider social considerations in making judgements in this area, as well as because of the autonomy allowed to judges in the civil law world, many of the lower courts have refused to accept these judgements as establishing precedents that are binding upon them (Sugeno 1979: 16). Moreover, some of the dissident judges have given as the reason for their refusals, not the dubious *Tokyo Central Post Office* formulation, but the simple unconstitutionality of the restrictions on public sector trade unionists (see the cases listed by Sugeno 1979: 37–8, n. 75).

CASE LAW II: COLLECTIVE EMPLOYMENT RELATIONS IN THE PRIVATE SECTOR

If the vast majority of the cases which have raised constitutional issues have related to the public sector, then an equally large preponderance of the cases that have resulted in more routine industrial relations issues coming before the courts have related to the private sector. However, the most interesting issues to have arisen as regards this sector have also done so because the right to organise, bargain and act collectively is a constitutional one even though the issues themselves have not involved decisions about the constitutionality or otherwise of particular acts. As was noted in Chapter 3, this right has proved to be somewhat double-edged as far as labour is concerned. Apart from the fact that in the private sector individuals may be forced to join a union irrespective of their individual wishes and/or commitments, the running together of the rights to organise, bargain and act collectively has meant that unorganised or dissident employees, including non-regular employees in otherwise organised companies, have few legal rights if they wish to act collectively or unofficially (for the relatively favourable position enjoyed by unorganised workers in the Unites States, see Bohlander 1987). On the other hand, the unambiguous nature of the manner in which these rights are specified and the ease with which a union may be organised has made it relatively easy for minority and even non-registered unions to survive, at least where the only threats to them have been legal ones.

It is this double-sidedness that has allowed the Trade Union Law to be both a source of support for, as well as resistance to, the establishment of *Kigyôshugi* in the workplace. The tolerance and even the encouragement exhibited as regards the post-entry closed shop has facilitated the creation of an appearance of communitarian enterprise as well as the disciplining of recalcitrant individuals who would lose their jobs if they lost their union membership (for the existence of some legal protection for individuals in such a position, see Hanami 1979: 94). Initially, the protection afforded minority unions also facilitated these developments in that the first wave of minority unions, those which emerged in the 1950s, largely consisted of unions that were keen to establish a closer and more cooperative relationship with the companies they were associated with. More recently, however, minority unions have tended to be animated by values that are antithetical to *Kigyôshugi*, with the result that their continued existence represents both an unwanted element of pluralism in some workplaces and a means whereby alternative visions of industrial relations might be articulated.

Perhaps the clearest evidence for the proposition that the Trade Union Act, as interpreted by the judiciary, has facilitated the spread of *Kigyôshugi*, may be provided by a consideration of both the legal tolerance afforded joint consultation and the uses to which joint consultation has been put. In the United States the existence of the National Labour Relations Act's insistence on union autonomy, as specified in its unfair labour practice provisions, has led to the judicial imposition of rather strict limits on union–management cooperation. It would appear that the existence of a very similar set of provisions in the Trade Union Act has had no such result. This suggests that the Japanese judiciary has read these provisions in the context of a rather different set of non-juridical discourses to those which have informed the readings provided by their American opposite numbers. More specifically, it suggests that the Japanese judiciary has read these provisions in the light of *Kigyôshugi* with its preference for harmony, rather than in the light of what I have termed elsewhere 'corporate liberalism' with its strong preference for the clear differentiation of management and labour rights (Woodiwiss 1990a: ch. 8).

In the same way that it may be argued that the American courts' response has had negative consequences in relation to the improvement of the relations between labour and capital (Gould 1984: 164–5), so it may also be argued that the Japanese courts' have failed to indicate much sensitivity to the complexities involved in the notion of industrial democracy. Of course, given *Kigyôshugi* and the effect that its presence has on how the term 'democracy' is understood (see p. 74), the latter should not be surprising. Indeed the body of case law and scholarly commentary presently under discussion provides a very clear instance of how unproblematically the fact of hierarchy may coexist alongside assertions of democracy. Thus the powerful assertion of the priority of the managerial prerogative with which the postwar judicial history of labour law opens is not seen to cause any problems when set beside authoritative commentary such as Hanami's, which states that:

> Japanese law...does not, in general, specify issues for bargaining which are compulsory or mandatory. Thus, in Japanese legal theory and in practice a wide range of issues are susceptible to collective bargaining: in fact almost all the issues over which the employer has any control are regarded as coming within the scope of bargaining. The argument of the 'management prerogative' has rarely been accepted – except by management ideologues.
>
> (Hanami 1979: 109)

The general issue of the managerial prerogative and whether or not it is qualified by joint consultation will be discussed further below (see p. 152). For now it is sufficient to note the following: first, that joint consultation, which provides the context within which most discussion about issues other than wages takes place, very seldom takes the form of bargaining; second, that when it does take the form of bargaining (e.g. in relation to transfers, redundancy and retirement), it is much more likely to involve issues of employee discipline than other management actions such as basic production and sales plans; third, that unions are almost always at a disadvantage in any such bargaining, because the sorts of issues it is most likely to relate to are generally those covered by the company works rules, which all employees have already acceded to as a condition of employment (see p. 140); and, finally, that authoritative case commentary also makes it clear that not even consultative agreements, let alone any 'understandings' that might have been arrived as regards the negotiability of such rules, are necessarily accepted as binding by the courts. In sum, joint consultation is better understood as a means of gaining union support for a company's disciplinary structure *vis-à-vis* its employees than as a means whereby a measure of industrial democracy is brought to the workplace. This is a point that gains still greater force once it is realised: first, that legally the collective agreement takes precedence over the individual contract of employment, even when the terms of the former are not as good as those of the latter (Hanami 1979: 113; for English moves in this direction, see Leader 1988); and second, that grievance procedures which include the possibility of outside arbitration are virtually unknown in Japanese workplaces (Sugeno n.d.: 14).

The topic whose discussion best illustrates this point is that of *shukko* (transfers to related firms), which is the point at which the patriarchal obligation to provide 'lifetime employment' comes into conflict with as well as contributes to the supposed harmony of the Japanese workplace. Today such transfers are among the chief means used by larger Japanese companies to avoid redundancies when faced by unfavourable market conditions and for this reason the requirement that employees accede to transfer orders is usually included in a company's works rules. (Sugeno [1989: 4] gives figures which indicate that nowadays between 6 and 8 per cent of employees are subject to *shukko* every year.) They make sense from the core company's point of view because they shift the burden of deciding what to do with surplus personnel to others and so protect both the core company's balance sheet and its personnel resources. Additionally, they enable the core company to hold on to trained personnel in the hope of better times to come. They make less sense from the point of view of employees since, because geographical movement and radical changes of job (e.g. from production work to sales) are often involved, they lead to considerable disruptions in their personal lives. Indeed, from the employees point of view transfers are most often resented: employees feel under great pressure to accept them owing to the rigidities in the labour market which means that there are few opportunities for employment in other large companies, especially for the older workers who are those most often chosen for transfer.

Thirty years ago transfers were very seldom challenged (Hanami 1979: 60), but today they are contested surprisingly often, which results in unions being placed in a very uncomfortable position, especially if transfers are among the issues about which they consult and/or bargain (i.e. the burden very often falls on them to try to convince the aggrieved individual that they should accept the transfer on pain of a dismissal that the union may not be willing or able to challenge, see *Toppan Insatsu Disciplinary Dismissal Incident* 1957). In sum, alongside the maintenance of a dual labour market and the institutionalisation of the temporary worker system, the enforcement of *shukko* is one of the principal ways in which employees have been made to play their part in the attainment of Japan's renowned flexibility.

Because of the *Kigyôshugi*-inspired importance of works rules and joint consultation, collective agreements tend to be very vague documents concerned only with generalities. The somewhat ironic result is that, although the Japanese courts have read into such agreements the assumption of 'a peace obligation' by both parties for the duration of the contract, in striking contrast to what happens in the United States they have very seldom found unions to be in breach of such an obligation even though employers have often asked them to try (see, for example, the reasons for the rejection of the 1977 petition for provisional disposition [the Japanese equivalent of injunctive relief] on behalf of Pan American World Airways Inc.; see also Gould 1984: 149–50, and Hanami 1979: 116).

Less accidentally, because it derives directly from the constitutional protection given to collective bargaining as well as from the broad definition of act of dispute contained in the Labour Relations Adjustment Law, Japanese unions also appear to enjoy a greater tactical freedom as to the means they may use to pursue their ends than their American and European counterparts. Moreover, as Hanami (1979: 119, 130) notes, their right to use the various acts of dispute at their disposal is stronger than the employers' right to resort to lockouts, since the latter does not enjoy constitutional protection.

All that said, there are nevertheless significant restrictions on the right to strike. These derive from the close specification of the purposes for which the right to engage in acts of dispute is to be found in the basic trade union laws (see pp. 111). On this basis the courts have typically found that 'political' strikes, etc. do not enjoy any greater legal protection in private industry than they do in the public sector. In addition, and more interestingly because this is an instance of the judicial discovery of an 'unfair labour practice' on labour's part (see p. 112), the courts have typically found that 'sympathy strikes' too are unprotected, in this instance because the employers in the sympathetically struck plants do not have the power to resolve the core dispute (*Mitsui Mining Co. Ltd. and seven others* v. *Japan Miners Labor Union and four others* 1957).

One great disadvantage suffered by enterprise unions, as contrasted to the national craft or industrial unions more typical of other societies, is their inability to build up substantial strike funds. For this reason Japanese strikes tend to be very short, often of only a few hours duration. As well as not finding their way into the strike statistics which only include strikes of longer than four hours, their place as *the* act of dispute is very often taken by such activities as picketing, working to rule, coordinated holiday taking, pasting up posters and, most unusually, wearing ribbons that specify not only the reasons for disputes, but also the protesting employees opinions of their employers. Because of this, any judgement as to the significance that should be attached to any latitude that employees have been granted in the use that they can make of such activities has to bear in mind that the unions depend upon them as surrogates for strike action.

In the past Labour Commissions and the courts tended to show greater toleration of such activities and indeed of violence than was the case, for example, in the United States (Fukui 1973).

This is no longer the case today. As was the case with public sector unions (see pp. 127–9), the period since the early seventies has seen a tightening up of the restrictions on private sector unions. For example, and again inspired by *Kigyôshugi*-type ideas as to the sorts of behaviour that are proper in Japanese companies, the courts have made it clear that any violence on a union's part will result not simply in criminal charges but also in an immediate loss of standing before the courts (*Kotobuki Architectural Research Company Case*, 1977). Similarly, but more recently, the courts have also shown themselves to be less tolerant as regards 'ribbon struggles'. When the Tokyo Local Labour Relations Commission considered the matter in the *Hotel Okura Case* (1972), it allowed that when a dispute was in progress the works rules were suspended and so it found nothing wrong with the staff's wearing of ribbons critical of the management. By contrast, when the Tokyo District Court considered the same case on appeal in 1975, it found that 'ribbon struggles were illegal in general'. The court's reasoning is particularly interesting in the present context, since its dependence on the discourse of *Kigyôshugi* is very clear. For this reason the judgement will be quoted at length:

> Participation of workers in a union activity such as ribbon struggle during working hours should be said to be opportunistic conduct of the sort to benefit oneself at the expense of another ([cf.] engaging in a *sumo* match using another's loincloth), and lacking in fairness....
>
> In the setting of a demonstration of solidarity shown by the so-called ribbon struggle, the operative principle is equality between labor and management, as with collective action such as collective bargaining and labor strikes (*domei higyo*). When the ribbon struggle is held during working hours, the operative relationship becomes unequal between the employer giving supervisory orders concerning work and the workers who must abide by work or profferment of labor. Thus the development of the ribbon struggle necessarily assumes the disparate qualities of unequal and equal relationships piled on top of each other. Looking at this from a psychological framework, for the worker while he is abiding by the employer's supervisory orders and working or proffering labor the

135

psychological structure of subordination and sincerity operates, whereas when demonstrating solidarity the psychological structure of antagonism and struggle prevails. Although these two aspects have a relationship of mutual opposition, their simultaneity causes them to function as a dual structure. In the case of the employer... the psychological structure of orders and demands operates, while when a demonstration of solidarity is made by ribbon struggle the psychological structure of hesitation and loss of power operates.

Neither labor nor management can avoid the feeling of disorder caused by the psychological dual structure functions such as those above. The effect of the psychological harassment of the employer by the tactic aimed at his nerves is especially great. The multiple accumulation of the effect of the ribbon struggle tactic causes anxiety over the erosion of the basis of the unequal relationship of giving orders and submitting to them between the employer and the workers. It should be said that the harmful effect of the emotional quality presented in the designation 'ribbon' has a depth which cannot possibly be fathomed, and leads to a threat upon the establishment of the employer's right to supervise work. In terms of its relationship to the workers, it is not without anxiety that the mechanism of psychological dual structure which on the one hand is obedient and on the other is antagonistic towards superiors divides the psychological operations of people who are logical beings, paving the way for the formation of split personalities. For the dignity of the character of labor, ribbon struggle is a tactic which should not be taken.

(*Hotel Okura Case* 1975: 12–13)

What one is presented with in this passage is a singularly explicit illustration of how *Kigyôshugi* has entered and restructured the discourse of labour law. The initial mention of *sumo* immediately indicates that what is being enunciated is an instance of *Nihonjinron*: in Japanese companies employers supervise and employees submit to this supervision with 'sincerity' and without question; in certain special situations, such as where collective bargaining is taking place, there is equality between labour and management; a ribbon struggle can have no place in such situations since, on the basis of impromptu psychological speculation (n.b. not on the basis of legal doctrine), it is argued that it not only undermines this equality but also threatens the acceptance of inequality that is basic to the employment relation, thereby causing anxiety amongst management and threatening to turn the labour force into a band of psychotics. In 1982 the Tokyo Labour Commission appealed to the Supreme Court. The Supreme Court upheld both the judgement and the reasoning of the lower court. The net result, then, of the entry of *Kigyôshugi* into the discourse of labour law has been to further reduce the anyway very restricted access that Japanese trade unions have to the means with which they may attempt to enforce their will.

At this point it would seem appropriate to ask whether or not the protections afforded unions by the unfair labour practice provisions of the Trade Union Act remain intact. Here the first point that has to be made is that today (*contra* Hanami 1979: 127) all of these protections are counter-balanced by judicially produced replications of all the unfair labour practices attributable to labour under the Taft–Hartley Act. Thus, like their American equivalents, Japanese unions are: (1) forbidden to interfere with employees rights to self-organisation (see the discussion of minority unions pp. 137–8); (2) forbidden to engage in sympathy strikes (see pp. 138–9); (3) forbidden to use violence and other unfair tactics (see the discussion of 'ribbon struggles' pp. 135–6); (4) forbidden to enforce a closed shop under certain circumstances (see, again, the discussion of minority unions p. 138). In other words, whatever the current condition of union protections they may no longer be construed in any sense as privileges. Despite what has just been said and although the spread of joint consultation has rendered the issue of managerial interference in union affairs a somewhat anachronistic one, the protections afforded to unions nevertheless appear to be in a pretty robust condition, especially where issues of discrimination because of union activities are concerned (Hanami 1979: 133–4; *Asahi Broadcasting Case* [1976]). The reason for this would appear to be that the Labour Commissions as well as the courts have had little choice but to insist on very literal readings of what are very unambiguous prohibitions. The same literalness has also recently but very belatedly enabled the courts to begin to support the claims of dissident trade union members (Sugeno 1988b: 4–8).

Apart from protecting individual trade unionists as such, this literalism has provided very significant support to the minority unions which exist in roughly 4 per cent of organised workplaces (Sugeno 1988a: 131). Minority union members as individuals have also been protected against discrimination on the basis of minority union membership (*The Japan Mail Order Case* 1975) and such unions themselves have successfully brought suits on the basis of company refusals to bargain. In 1983, 37 per cent of all the unfair labour practice cases filed with local labour commissions involved minority unions, and as far as companies employing more than 500 employees were concerned fully 66 per cent of such cases involved minority unions (Sugeno 1988a: 131). However, the protection afforded minority unions was dramatically reduced in 1985, when the Supreme Court decided the *Nissan Motor Company Case*. Although the case itself was won by the minority union involved, the Court took the opportunity to enunciate for the first time the principles it thought should control in such cases, and these are likely to prove much less favourable to minority unions than those which have informed commission and lower court judgements until now. Whereas what is known as the 'neutrality obligation' used to be interpreted very literally, it now seems that it may be qualified in the light of the relative strengths of the coexisting unions. In addition, the Court argued, an employer's mere insistence on making the minority union the same offer as the majority union ought no longer to be considered, *ipso facto*, an attempt to manipulate negotiations as had tended to be the case in the past (Sugeno 1988a).

Although this decision appears to involve a radical change of doctrine, it is important to note that it is in line with a much older decision, which first made plain Japanese law's *Kigyōshugi*-inspired preference for what Sugeno terms 'autonomous' company/enterprise union negotiations (cf. section 4(3) of the original PCLL, see pp. 115–16). Ironically, the case concerned was also one that the unions won, namely the *Goka Roren (Chemical Workers Confederation) Case* of 1960. Reflecting the moves towards more centralised bargaining implicit in the then only recently adopted *shunto* strategy, a group of enterprise unions in the chemical industry demanded that officials from the federation to which they belonged should be allowed to participate in their negotiations with their employers, who were also organised into a federation. The employers refused to accept this demand and as a consequence the unions complained to their local and ultimately to the Central Labour Commission that this constituted an unfair refusal to bargain. The Central Labour Commission found for the unions not on such grounds as that the realities of bargaining had changed, but on the far narrower ones that the power to negotiate had been properly assumed by the federation because in this instance the federation had played a useful role in the previous year's negotiations.

In comparative terms, this decision may be judged to have imposed rather strict limits on the involvement of third parties in negotiations between companies and unions. Commenting on this case, Gould puts the point in a way that draws attention to the importance of *Kigyôshugi* not only in this decision but also in the discourses of production more generally:

> some of the federations do engage in collective bargaining, jointly with negotiators from the affiliated unions. This is the case in the coal mining, and privately owned railways, for example. But they are aberrations in the [sic] Japanese collective bargaining. Employers and workers prefer that outsiders be excluded from the 'family' or 'home' (*uchi*).
> (Gould 1984: 119)

In sum and as of this writing, *Kigyôshugi* has succeeded in reducing considerably the pluralism implicit in the amended Trade Union Law and to a significant degree it has reconstructed the law in its own unitary image. It remains to be seen whether or not the encouragement recently given to union democracy represents the beginning of a pluralistic fracturing of this image.

CASE LAW III: INDIVIDUAL EMPLOYMENT RELATIONS

As mentioned above, individual labour law is almost entirely a postwar creation in Japan. This said, it does not mean that individual labour law is any freer of the signs of patriarchalism than any other part of the labour law edifice. The Supreme Court has quite recently taken to finding employment contracts where their existence has been denied, in order that it may apply the Trade Union Law (*Kanagawa Labour Relations Commission and*

Yuken Manufacturing Company Ltd v. *National Union of General Workers* 1976). However, because Japanese labour law, individual and collective, is of a piece and is also largely a statutory creation, it cannot be said, as Kahn-Freund famously said of the individual contract of employment in English law, that it is 'the cornerstone of the edifice'. Nevertheless, a lot may be learned about the particularity of Japan's labour law by considering the way in which the individual's relation to her or his employer is legally constituted and regulated.

The suggestion made earlier (p. 122) that individual institutions might become laws unto themselves as far as the constitutional rights of individuals were concerned may be repeated with respect to their contractual rights. There was no need for an equivalent to *Tokachi Girls' Commercial High School*, which was the case that opened the way for the entry of *Kigyôshugi* into collective labour law, since the door was left unlocked in one of the original trio of labour laws, namely the Labour Standards Law. The pertinent provisions of the Law are those that specify that all establishments employing ten or more workers should draw up a set of works rules in consultation with the labour force, which should then be checked and approved by the Ministry of Labour. Because Japanese collective agreements have a relatively narrow scope and are typically confined to such issues as wages, bonuses, retirement benefits and hours of work, the works rules

> legally and practically...represent the major norm establishing rules and conditions of employment in Japanese workplaces.
>
> (Sugeno, n.d.: 3)

Although ministry vetting assures that certain minimum standards are observed, the way in which the courts have come to understand the legal significance of the rules has meant that it has become very difficult for individual employees in unorganised workplaces to assure themselves of any conditions that are better than the minimum. This is also true in many organised workplaces, since these rules provide the framework within which joint consultation takes place (see the discussion of transfers p. 132). According to Ohta, in the *Shuhoko Bus Case* (1968) the courts adopted what he terms 'the legal theory' as opposed to 'the contractual theory' of works rules:

> The legal theory regards works rules not as part of the contract of employment but as part of the law of the enterprise which each employee accepts when he joins it. Like society, every organisation, if it is not to become anarchic, must have its own laws, and will generate them spontaneously. An employee submits to these laws voluntarily by the fact of taking up work in an enterprise and must adhere to them...this act is not a contractual act.
>
> (Ohta 1988: 630)

The result is that the courts now accept unilateral changes to works rules made by companies even if they involve a worsening of conditions, provided only that such changes are 'reasonable' and/or reflect 'special circumstances'.

In order to bring this section to a close, I would like to briefly consider the single most important source of court actions in the area of individual labour law, namely dismissals, which account for nearly half of all labour suits in any year (Sugeno n.d.: 9). Here, the single most striking fact is how few such cases there are, despite the further fact that it is the amended Civil Code, which provides the pertinent controlling principles and which might be expected to be rather more resistant to *Kigyôshugi* than the labour laws. This has resulted in the courts' adoption of a rather strict 'good cause' test, which until recently has tended to favour the employee (Hanami 1979: 83, but see also *Toyo Sanso Joint Stock Company Case* 1979, where the criteria applied as regards economic causes were significantly relaxed). In 1983, only 611 applications were made to the courts for either provisional relief or judgement, whereas in Britain in the same year and out of a labour force that is less than half the size of Japan's roughly 35,000 unfair dismissal cases were heard by industrial tribunals (Komiya 1986: 31, 47). The reasons for this difference include the time-consuming nature and the great expense of Japanese legal proceedings (for example, in one case an appellant who took her protest against a reprimand to the Supreme Court was accompanied by 53 lawyers, *Fuji Heavy Industry Case* 1977). This said, the ultimate reason would appear to be *Kigyôshugi*. As Komiya puts it:

social and moral pressures also prevent the dismissed employee from taking legal action. Namely, the employee and the people surrounding him think, except in very extraordinary circumstances, that assertion of his rights before the public is disgraceful. The employee is also afraid that others might regard his personality as being unsuitable to harmonious group life and therefore that he might be excluded from other possible good jobs.

(Komiya 1986: 33)

Fortunately, some individuals do manage to cast aside these concerns, with the result that, for example, being drunk and entering another person's house in search of a toilet no longer represents grounds for dismissal (*Yokahama Rubber Case* 1970). Unfortunately, refusing to work overtime to which one's union has agreed and to which there is no legal limit (Hanami 1979: 65) is still a disciplinary offence that can be punished by dismissal (see The Joint Committee of Trade Unions Supporting Mr Tanaka's Trial 1989).

CONCLUSION

The answer to the question as to how and on what basis legal decisions have been made in the postwar period has been answered by demonstrating how the patriarchalism intrinsic to *Kigyôshugi* has ensured the constitutionality of some of the more questionable statutory articles and transformed the conception of the employment relationship that was basic to both the New Constitution and the Trade Union Union Law. In this way, then, the judiciary has played a significant role not only in the reinforcement of the statutory restrictions on the possibility that labour might use its civil rights as surrogate political rights (i.e. the legislative pre-defining of the ends of collective bargaining and the proliferation of sector-specific labour laws), but also in what is in my view the consequently unsurprising derogation of the basic trade union rights. The first effect was explicitly present in those cases where the incident which brought what was typically a public sector union to court was a protest against some aspect of government policy. It was also implicitly present, in the sense of being both a cause and an additional consequence of many of the judgements that contributed to the second effect.

Examples of the latter judgements include those which resulted in restrictions on what was allowable as an 'act of dispute', as well as those in which surrogates for unfair labour practices on labour's part (e.g. sympathy strikes) were created.

Limited by *Kigyôshugi*, as labour's rights now are, they nevertheless still represent the single most substantive set of limits to its hegemony. These are the limits which are undermined, whether they realise it or not, by those who make or repeat the claims made on behalf of supposedly egalitarian community-type or *mura*-type companies and argue, like Dore (1987) and Kuwahara (1988; 1989), that such companies are comparable to employee-managed enterprises in the west. (For earlier and less sanguine views that have retained their pertinence, see Taira 1970: pt 2; Nakayama 1975: 235 ff.) When produced by Japanese writers, such claims often conclude with the suggestion that the existing labour law anachronistically assumes that industrial relations are necessarily adversarial, hence its protectiveness towards minority unions, and that it should be recast so as to exclude such disruptive elements and so reflect and reinforce the actual cooperativeness of industrial relations. For example, the very prominent academic labour lawyer and public Labour Commission member Professor Sugeno (1988a: 35) chooses to end his discussion of the supposed emergence of a new and 'cooperative' rather than a conflictual industrial relations system with a quotation from a colleague, which discloses the assumption upon which this belief is based:

There are many scholars who advocate that since the current industrial relations are in a critical situation, we must take a direction to cope with it. Isn't it that they have tacitly presupposed the theory of class and capitalism of the 19th century as a sort of inertia from the past? I think that Japan has already detached herself completely from the structure of the pattern of the 19th century West, particularly in terms of class structure.

The suggestion that those aspects of the existing labour law which seek to assure minority unions' rights and by implication union autonomy more generally might be becoming an anachronism comes close to making explicit the view which has always been implicit in *Kigyôshugi*, namely the belief that unions of any type are not necessary where what are supposed to be the uniquely unique *ie* or *mura*-type institutions exist.

The authors of these claims seem to be unaware that the pertinence of the distinction between owners and non-owners extends considerably beyond the issue of financial control which they stress and extends to the distribution of all roles and functions as between executive management and the remainder of the labour force (cf. Edelman 1980: 53–4). Moreover, it is the maintenance of the distinction between owners and non-owners which has ensured that this distribution has not been modified except in regard to relatively marginal particulars and because of the existence of a degree of union independence which is itself in part dependent upon the possibility that a minority union might appear and challenge the incumbent union.

6

INDUSTRIAL RELATIONS, CLASS STRUCTURE AND THE SIGNIFICANCE OF RELUCTANT RECOGNITION

The answer to the question as to what have been the consequences of the system of labour law whose operation has just been described is very simple. Although Japanese trade unions are, speaking comparatively, by no means the unions least likely to engage in acts of dispute, because other acts are more common than strikes and because the latter when they occur tend to be very short, Japanese industrial relations have in general been characterised by a very low level of disruption (Hanami 1979: 121 ff.). As with all other labour law systems, these disciplinary consequences are not explainable by reference to law alone. Reference must also be made to the political, economic, ideological and class balances between labour and capital institutionalised in the JES and the *shunto*. What the unions' achievements, the political resilience of the leftwing parties and the slight shift in the terms of the hegemonic ideology suggest sociologically is that the balances between the contending embodiments of the class structure have become very much more equal than they were before the war. However, as is also clear from the sustained political dominance of the LDP, from the slightness of the ideological shift and from the declining proportion of the labour force organised into unions, these balances have continued to be markedly more favourable to the embodiments of capital than to those of labour. Thus today unions are largely confined to the primary manufacturing and the former public sectors, and even there they encounter and are in part enclosed and socially confined by a legally sanctioned company level patriarchalism, and by a similarly legally sanctioned privileging of regular and/or unionised employees, which together

145

repeat and reinforce the national level constraints on unions and labour more generally.

In order to understand why this happened and the contribution of labour law to this outcome, it is necessary to combine the answers to the three questions posed at the beginning of this part and in so doing to look more closely at class relations at the workplace level. (For discussions of macro level class relations, see Ishida 1988; Ishida, Goldthorpe and Erikson 1988; Steven 1983). At the micro level a variety of forms of class relations, varying from the simple to the complex may be descried. In the advanced capitalist societies of the postwar world this variation in forms has been closely associated with size, with the result that these forms vary along a continuum. At one end of this continuum the simple form may be discerned amidst the relations that characterise small enterprises, whilst at the other end the complex form may be discerned amidst the relations which characterise large enterprises.

In small enterprises the boundary between the classes is readily apparent at the level of their embodiments.[1] The rights and powers of capital are centralised, have a restricted purview and result in the unambiguous positioning of somebody or some partners as the proprietor(s) and some other bodies as wage-labourers. In the case of large companies the boundary between the classes is very difficult to discern at the level of their embodiments. The rights and powers of capital are widely distributed both within and without the enterprise, and their purview in terms of the complexity of the activities and operations that are organised in terms of them is very extensive. The result is that it is extremely difficult to see how they may be understood to position an individual, a board of directors or even a supposed entity like 'top management' in such a way as to differentiate them unambiguously from other sections of the labour force. In such institutional settings and therefore in societies where such settings are frequently to be found, the importance of the class structure as the major and direct source of the positionings that determine the life-chances of individuals has been considerably reduced and partially displaced by other, although by no means unrelated, sources of positionings such as education, religion, race or company loyalty.

It is important, however, to emphasise that this reduction should in no way be taken as being indicative of the disappearance of capitalist class relations. The continued existence of the latter is utterly indifferent to the manner in which the positionings derived from it come to be embodied by particular human subjects or groups thereof. What this reduction does indicate, however, is the occurrence of an undermining of some at least of the commonalities which in the past have provided the bases upon which solidarities have been constructed between the embodiments of labour power. To be more specific, some have been separated out on the grounds of one or other non-class criteria and rewarded relatively highly, so that as the members of a supposed 'middle class' they may perform some of the labour necessary to the assembly, deployment and utilisation of capital.

KIGYOSHUGI AND THE DENIAL OF CLASS

Despite the particularities of Japan's postwar economic, political and ideological development, the range of forms of capitalist class relations just outlined may be discerned without difficulty in Japanese enterprises. However, as in most if not quite all other advanced capitalist societies, strenuous efforts have been and still are made by those positioned wholly or in part by capital to deny that the inequalities between them and those less fortunately positioned are intrinsic to the capitalist mode of production. However, what is different about the Japanese case, thanks to the pervasiveness of *Kigyôshugi*, and what vindicates the analytical stance taken in the present text as regards the ongoing relatively autonomous development of the class structure's conditions of existence, is the manifest pertinence of the fact that as it has developed the discourse which carries the denial of class has remained of a piece with and indeed central to that which carries the national identity. This has had the result that accepting one's position in one's *kaisha* has come to appear as equivalent to accepting one's position in society and vice versa. The two levels of discourse have thus continued to reinforce one another and thus remained a formidable source of resistance to the influence of alternative discourses such as those normally thought to be intrinsic to trade unionism or socialism and which are anyway defined by *Kigyôshugi* as alien.

In smaller companies, as on the farms, the pertinent protective discourse of class denial remains the traditional patriarchalist one whose critical elements are the ideas of *ie*, employer responsibility and employee loyalty (Bennett and Ishino 1963). In the years since the ending of the war, it may be safely assumed that this discourse has lost some of its disciplinary effectivity as job mobility has increased amongst smaller companies, as the skills required within them have been enlarged and enhanced (Koike 1988: ch. 5), as wage levels have approached those in the larger companies (Friedman 1988: ch. 4), as state-provided welfare facilities of all kinds have been improved (Maruo in Rose and Shiratori 1986), as women and minorities have slowly become more assertive (Cook and Hayashi 1980; Upham 1987) and, finally, as sources of capital for new small businesses apart from the traditional ones (parents, in-laws and ambitious/grateful employers) have become available (Friedman 1988: ch.5; Patrick and Rohlen 1987). Of course, the discourse of patriarchalism may still be heard in the smaller workplaces (Kondo 1990: chs 3, 5), and its applicability within them is still asserted by journalistic as well as academic commentators. It may also be assumed, although somewhat less safely, that its place at the centre of workplace discourse has been taken by the much more diffuse and abstract *Kigyôshugi* variant, which is broadcast by such commentators, and which gives a particular cast to the always subordinate, more straightforwardly calculative discourse of 'self-reliance', 'opportunity', etc., which Japanese working people, of course, share with their equivalents in other advanced capitalist societies (see p. 87). Sometimes this global patriarchalism is supported by the Buddhism of Sokagakkai, and about as often it is challenged by trade unionism, socialism or communism (Curtis 1988: 24–30).

In larger companies the pertinent protective discourse of class denial is far more elaborate than in the smaller ones, as has been made clear in a wide variety of studies (e.g. Allinson 1975; Abegglen and Stalk 1985; Clark 1979; Dore 1973; Gordon 1985; Hirschmeier and Yui 1981; Koike 1988; Inagami 1988; Levine 1958). Although *Kigyôshugi* scholars like Nakane and Murakami very consciously use originally feudal terms like *oyabun, kobun* and *mura*, to refer to the social relations to be found in large Japanese enterprises, in fact most of the features which distinguish them from their smaller counterparts and indeed from their overseas equivalents are the products of postwar developments. Large Japanese companies are extremely hierarchical and proudly acknowledge themselves so to be. However, in two senses they are often also claimed and claim themselves to be classless: first, in the sense that promotion within them depends upon seniority and merit rather than family background or inherited position; and second, in the sense that Japanese companies are supposedly organic wholes and hence not marked by the same class antagonisms as western companies.

Concerning promotion, the vast majority of new members of the larger Japanese companies join straight from either school or university and are assigned to a white or blue collar career, or in the case of women, non-career, tracks according to their level of education. Although there are some opportunities for jumping tracks for shopfloor workers, new entrants generally progress as cohorts along the tracks to which they were initially assigned, according to seniority and, increasingly, according to merit. However, because the hierarchy which they are ascending eventually becomes markedly pyramidal in shape, the proportion of the cohort rising to its topmost levels is rather low. Those who fail to make the rank of managing director or higher and thus to join the managing committee (*jomukai*) are generally satisfied and indeed considered satisfactory if, within fourteen years or so, they make the rank of *kacho* (section chief) or, more recently, become one of the '*tantomin*' (people in charge of something), which are regarded as the middle-management career grades. Thus the blue-collar/white-collar divide remains an important determinant of 'life-chances' (Vogel 1963). However, as befits organisations which aspire to be what Murakami has termed 'homo-functional', strenuous efforts are made to counter any explicit antagonisms between capital and labour, let alone any that might create the possibility of solidarities between blue- and white-collar employees.

Many companies espouse 'company philosophies', which explicitly deny the existence of even the possibility of such antagonisms and, because they often take the form of a statement of the founding patriarch's personal philosophy, they tend to acquire a quasi-sacred status; as an example, consider Matsushita Konosuke's oft repeated 'little lecture':

Don't think I run this company [Matsushita Electric]. Each of you has a part to play in its management. We need the ideas, skill, and knowledge of everyone to make a reservoir

149

of wisdom for more efficient operations, better product and service quality, and effective management. We have a good future if we can work that way.

(Matsushita 1984: 52)

In the same way that there are great similarities between these company philosophies, so there are great similarities in the ways in which they are put into practice, pronounced enough indeed that they are commonly referred to collectively as 'The Japanese Employment System'. In addition, as is consistent with their role in *Kigyôshugi*, these techniques of class denial are often referred to with traditional terms. For example, among the most common of these techniques is the practice of pre-meeting lobbying, which is greatly dignified by having the term *nemawashi* (the root-binding necessary when moving a tree) used to refer to it. Again, the more specifically Japanese practice of circulating and gaining support for suggestions originating in the lower ranks before they are submitted to superiors is similarly dignified by using the term *ringi-sho*, which is an ancient term of art in Japanese politics. Finally, the terms used to refer to the different components of wages and salaries – *nenko* (seniority), *shokuno* (ability) and bonus – all continue to connote the prewar patriarchalist/paternalistic management and payment system in which they originated as discretionary payments (Gordon 1985), despite the fact that nowadays, at least where unions are present, they are generally the subject of negotiation. The ideological effect of all of this is sometimes reinforced by referring to the system so constructed as 'Confucian' in some ill-defined sense.

In Japan as elsewhere, the term trade union evokes an antithetical discourse to that of patriarchalism. However, for reasons which are in part fortuitous and which were spelt out in Chapters 4 and 5, the consequences to the presence of this sign in the workplace are not as disruptive to the dominance of the discourses of class-denial as might at first be imagined. Quite accidentally the typical union in the private sector is the enterprise union. Quite accidentally also, Japan's postwar labour law allows all supervisors up to those *kacho* who have authority in the personnel sphere to be members of the same union. Finally, and again quite accidentally, the same body of law allows and even supports the possibility of dual unionism.

Not so accidentally, the possibilities inherent in this combination of circumstances were eventually grasped by employers as they contended with the often militant unions of the 1950s. As a result, employers sometimes took advantage of strike situations by encouraging the formation of second, more moderate and often white-collar-led unions, and then settling with them on favourable terms (Cole 1971; Gordon 1985: ch.10; Shimodaira 1985; Totsuka 1984). Very often this had disastrous consequences for the unions which initiated the strikes as well as an inhibiting effect on other unions. Again not so accidentally and as permitted by the law, companies are free to and usually do provide favoured unions with offices and all the other equipment and facilities they require in order to perform their role, e.g. automatic dues check-off, the post-entry closed shop and time-off for conducting union business. In a society where knowledge of the purpose and effects of such pre-giving is a critical part of its day-to-day fabric, the significance of such a set of gestures is particularly clear. Moreover, the possibility that the expectations of union behaviour thus encouraged might be disappointed is minimised by the unions' legally supported participation in consultative committees, by the enlistment of their support for after-hours quality circle activity, and by the exclusion of outsiders, whether from employers' associations or from the trade union federations, from collective bargaining sessions. Finally, all of the relations between the two sides are conducted in the context of such ritualistic and implicit denials of class difference as are represented by the requirements that all employees, regardless of rank, sometimes wear the same uniform, sometimes eat in the same canteen and sometimes attend the same social activities, as well as in the context of shared dependencies upon the company for health, welfare, housing, 'lifetime employment' and even friendships and marriage partners.

CONCLUSION

Although it has thus far turned out to be to capital's advantage, the fact that Japanese labour law allows many supervisory staff to be members of the same union as ordinary employees means that it also represents a seldom acknowledged, but everpresent, latent threat to the security of capital's control over the labour process – white- and blue-collar employees may unite to oppose top management. It seems to me, therefore, that, regardless of why company members think it is present, the critical and, for capital, the most valued general consequence of the entry of *Kigyôshugi* into labour law and the discourses of production is the way in which, in addition to weakening labour's ability to mount possessory challenges, it has also contributed to the blurring of the dividing line between blue- and white-collar labour and so to a reduction in the visibility and the possible significance of any divisions in the workplace – 'unite and rule' rather than 'divide and rule' would appear to be the principle which has come to inform the strategy of Japanese management as the JES has matured. A strategy which the judiciary has felt it necessary to reinforce with special rigour since the early 1970s, perhaps because of an increased restiveness on the part of the embodiments of the so-called middle class as is most clearly exemplified by their support for citizens' movements at the same time. In sum, the consequence of the articulation of the balances just outlined with a labour law system which has become ever more strongly marked by *Kigyôshugi* has been the production of a set of discourses of production wherein, at every point at which a union might have assumed or asserted a difference between labour and capital, the company has already said *'kaisha'* and the union has already agreed.

All that said, the discourses and techniques of class denial cannot obscure the following: (1) that joint consultation committees have very little say in, and certainly do not allow for, *negotiations* in such critical areas as strategic policy, organisational change, the introduction of new technology, hiring policies, employee transfers, health and safety, training, welfare and finally even cultural and sports policies (Inagami 1988: 25, table 6); (2) that trade unions retain a certain legally supported autonomy; and (3) that collective bargaining is substantially affected by the norms established during the *shunto* (Takanashi 1989; Levine 1982: 49 ff.). In other words, the exigencies arising from capitalist class relations continue to have a determinative effect upon the actual and possible relations between the embodiments of capital and labour. Despite their relative freedom from shareholder control, Japanese managers cannot give up more than a very restricted quantum of their rights and powers of possession and control – strikingly, the rights and powers of title are seldom if ever mentioned whether in the context of union–management discussions or in academic/journalistic commentary upon them. Nevertheless, thanks to the unambiguous nature of some of their legal rights, their establishment of economic and political organisations, and despite the immense effort that has been put into their pacification, Japanese working people still remain dependent upon their possession of these sources and instruments of power if they are to continue to remain able to set and pursue their own industrial agenda.

In the end, then, it is the persistence of these class–structural effects which makes so dubious Murakami's picture of the *kaisha* as a 'homo-functional hierarchy' as well as all other representations of it as some sort of post-capitalist, communitarian organisation comparable to western employee-managed companies. My guess is that this is a judgement which will repeated more often if (or when) Japan receives further shocks (a third oil shock, or a collapse in property values, for example) and as the JES anyway becomes frayed at the edges in response to a changing macro-economic environment, whose challenges are summarised in the phrases 'the strong yen' and 'the hollowing out of the economy', and which *should* result in the overcoming of the current labour shortage, at least in the larger companies. To be more specific, 'half-a-lifetime-employment' becomes more frequent, as enterprise unions lose their bargaining and protective effectiveness as regards 'regular' employees (Tabata 1989), as the proportion of temporary and part-time employees in large companies increases, as the labour shortage persists in smaller and medium-sized companies, and, relatedly, as organising opportunities for minority and/or general unions increase (Aoki 1987; Japan Institute of Labour 1983, 1988; Kamata 1983; Kawanishi 1986; Osawa 1988; Shimada 1980, 1988). Indeed this may already be happening, as is suggested by the increase which has been observed over the past ten years or so in the proportion of labour law cases which arise in large enterprises with minority unions and in the medium-sized companies where the JES has always been less developed. Moreover, it is possible that the gap between white- and blue-collar workers may in the long run prove to be less socially divisive than it is in other advanced capitalist societies. This is because, in addition to shared union membership, the levels of perquisites (Woronoff 1983) and the educational differences between the two groups are far less marked in Japan.

153

It might also be that the sense of economic grievance engendered by and reflected in these and other developments (e.g. evidence of increasing inequality and the introduction of a new consumption tax), and shared by wage and salary earners alike, may have been powerfully reinforced by the impact on party loyalties of the scandals which have recently beset the Liberal Democratic Party. All in all, what with these developments, the uniting of all of the non-Communist unions in a new organisation (Shin Rengo) and the Socialist Party's grasping of at least some of the levers of state power, it is just possible that in the not too distant future the world may begin to hear about a rather different Japan as compared to that which has recently been the source of so many one-sided lessons. In which case, the employee's often proud talk of 'his/her company' might be about to take on a more explicitly proprietorial air and *Kigyôshugi* a rather different signification (cf. Kondo 1990: 218 ff.).

NOTE

1 The remainder of this section is a revised version of a part of Woodiwiss 1990c.

CONCLUSION: VARIETIES OF CAPITALIST LAW, CITIZENSHIP RIGHTS AND THE QUESTION OF POSTMODERNISM

The principal substantive point made in this study has been that an examination of the wider social context within which Japanese industrial relations have developed discloses a certain social–structural resistance to the acceptance of the existence of independent and assertive trade unions, a resistance whose roots run far deeper than the LDP's postwar political supremacy. This is a resistance sufficient to require one to qualify the standard view of Japanese trade unions as having achieved full legal and social recognition by an insistence on a continuing reluctance which still attaches to their acceptance as fully legitimate participants in Japanese society, capable of enforcing their civil and other rights by means of what Marshall termed 'a sort of secondary industrial citizenship'. More specifically, it has been suggested that the deeper sources of this resistance and reluctance may be found in the enhancement and transformed persistence of certain characteristics of prewar Japanese society: i.e. in the enhanced dominance of capitalist relations of production; in the continuing dualism of the economy; in the continuing primacy of the bureaucracy within the ensemble of state institutions; in the continuing patriarchalism of the hegemonic ideology; and, finally, in the continuing social marginality of the law. In what follows I will return to the last of these once more in order to explain why it has been of such critical significance.

VARIETIES OF CAPITALIST LAW

Properly capitalist law (i.e. law with its axis around the primacy of the specifically capitalist mode of possession of property in the means of production, Woodiwiss 1990b: ch. 7) did not exist

155

in Japan until the promulgation of the 1889 Constitution and the activation of the Civil Code in 1898. And even then, it took a far from pure form, with the result that the more general powers of the state, rather than any specifically 'legal' notions, were more pertinent and were, therefore, what allowed and legitimated the most significant of the state interventions in industrial relations that took place in the pre–1945 period. Notwithstanding the existence, beginning in 1889, of an explicit constitutional right to freedom of association, collectivities of industrial workers first became and largely remained known to the courts as the perpetrators of crimes against the state rather than of civil injuries to the owners of capital; i.e. the legal issue remained the legitimacy of combinations of labourers as such, rather than that of their demands. In this regard there is a striking difference between the Japanese experience and that of some but by no means all western labour movements. Although, in the face of capitalist antipathy, any early legal toleration allowed to or achieved by trade unions seldom remained unchallenged for long anywhere, the juridical means found to define the limits of toleration were equally seldom the *raison d'état* so often invoked in Japan. In other societies the arrival of a legal basis for the toleration of collective labour actions (i.e. a right to freedom of association in the workplace) meant that such *raison d'état* as were present in the Common Law's conspiracy doctrine could no longer achieve a result in a court, whether thanks to the passage of statutes, as in Britain, or to the ingenuity of judges, as in the United States. This was because of the contradiction that would have had to have been present in legal reasoning for it to have been otherwise – either freedom of association existed or it did not. In Britain and the United States, then, the arrival of an explicit right to freedom of association meant that, if restrictions were sought to the extent of this freedom, civil means had to be found to limit it rather than criminal and political means to prohibit it.

It is impossible to differentiate 'capitalist law' from what I have termed elsewhere 'democratic capitalist law' (Woodiwiss 1990a: ch. 5) in relation to Britain and the United States. In the latter societies the law became properly 'capitalist' only once the law of the market entered the sphere of production, only once, in other words, the relationship between employer and employee had become contractual rather than one of master and servant. This in turn only occurred once the state had become representative of more than simply the property-owning section of the population (Woodiwiss 1990b: 118).

In sum and because of either political bargaining or political calculation, the following syllogism became constitutive of British and American law as systematised discursive entities, and as a consequence imparted what has been in comparative terms a privileged degree of protection to the employment relation – if freedom of association means that the state cannot treat association as a crime, and if freedom of association reaches the employment relation, then the state can find no crime in any instance of association in the workplace which is not for a purpose which is otherwise criminal. The result has been that, with the variable exception of some public employees, the state may only intervene indirectly in the workplace by attempting to enforce the employment contract (e.g. through injunctions) or by statutorily altering the general form of the employment contract (e.g. by insisting on the inclusion or exclusion of certain conditions). Put another way, in Britain and the United States, provided the conditions necessary for contractual validity have been fulfilled, the employment contract always was and still is regarded as an essentially private relation. This remains the case even when a union is present, despite the state's increasing interest in its content, and despite the fact that, thanks to the presence of 'public interest' considerations in legal discourse, the anti-union preferences present in especially the hegemonic ideology of the United States have long affected its content (Woodiwiss 1990b: ch. 8).

LAW AND THE ENFORCEMENT OF CITIZENSHIP RIGHTS

In Japan, as in several continental European societies, but in the context of a political and ideological regime which has consistently been far more hostile to labour, no such privilege has ever attached to the employment relation. My argument has been that the reason for this, again as in the same European societies, was that Japanese law was capitalist long before the society was democratic. This was so whether one considers its state form or its dominant ideology. Capital's freedoms were secured by a state-centred legal system articulated with a patriarchalist ideology, rather than by a property-centred 'rule of law' articulated

157

with a liberal democratic ideology (cf. Henderson's [1968b: 415] distinction between 'rule by law' and 'rule of law'). This had important consequences both for how these freedoms were secured and for the general nature of the law/society relation. Given the reinvention of Japan's patriarchalist ideology and the specific nature of Japan's variant of 'capitalist law', nothing in the postwar reforms has succeeded in imposing on the society's lawmakers, whether legislative of judicial, an obligation to extend the same gift of privacy to parties to employment contracts as they have extended freely, if not without some concern in some quarters, to parties to other types of contract. 'Freedom of contract', rather than 'freedom of the employment contract', was and remains the constitutive principle of Japan's legal system.

The result, so far from making Japan's the 'voluntarist' industrial relations system *par excellence*, which is the extraordinary claim made by Hanami and Blanpain (1989: 13), has been that the employment relation in Japan has been far more open to the attentions of the state and far more susceptible to the incantations of the hegemonic ideology than has been the case in Britain or even the United States. Moreover, this has had consequences that have been far less favourable to labour than has been the case where similar developments have occurred in the more statist of western European societies. This is because in the latter, thanks to the political successes of social–democratic parties, union-supportive ideas have become embedded in the hegemonic discourses. Thus the Japanese labour movement finds itself, like its American cousin, in the worst of all possible worlds. Despite its relatively privileged legal status, it lacks the social acceptance enjoyed by all western European labour movements, whilst, in part because of this status, it also lacks that capacity to act in the militant defence of its rights which from time to time has been exhibited by the British labour movement.

Because the law/society relation is a two-way street, as well as for more abstract theoretical reasons (Woodiwiss 1990b: pt 3), I wholly agree with and have tried to act upon Upham's (1987: 218) recent conclusion that if one is to understand this relation in Japan (or anywhere else for that matter), one has to examine not only the ways in which society affects the law, but also the ways in which the law affects society. The principal point of difference between us is a matter of emphasis which reflects the very different conceptions of law which inform our analyses, as well as, perhaps, the different areas of substantive law which we have examined. Putting the point very briefly, I am far more insistent than Upham that what I have termed 'patriarchalism' and he has termed an elite preference for 'particularism and informality' not only explains the widespread cultural deprecation of the law but also permeates all aspects of Japanese law. For this reason, all those who seek the legislative redress, which Upham correctly insists is more worthwhile than many other observers (western as well as Japanese) have been prepared to grant, should be prepared to pay very close attention indeed to the drafting of the pertinent texts. The purpose would be to ensure that they be made as resistant as possible to the patriarchalist readings which one may be certain the judiciary and other authoritative readers will attempt, most probably without realising it, to impose upon them. In the absence of such attention and as is sadly exemplified by the recent law concerning sexual discrimination in the workplace, all their efforts to secure the rights of the citizenry are likely to fall prey to those 'subtler pressures' of which Maruyama wrote and which, in the name of duty and in the absence of much in the way of a countervailing 'secondary industrial citizenship', I have suggested constrain the rights of trade unionists still.

As John Goldthorpe (1964) argued so many years ago, although Japan may not be of the same phenotype as other advanced capitalist societies it is most definitely of the same genotype irrespective of the aspect – economic, political or ideological – at which one looks. And this is because in Japan, as anywhere else capitalist relations of production exist, certain conditions, including certain ideological ones, have to be met if capitalism is to exist.[1] The difference between the Japanese case, its European and even its American equivalents is that, both because of the persistence of certain structural continuities and because of certain historical accidents, those ideologically and legally identified as the possessors of property in the means of production have seldom been seriously challenged as regards either the use they make of their property or their possession, control and title to it. In sum, the various particularistic, pseudo-collectivist and patriarchalist discourses which have been successively hegemonic, and which have helped capitalist possession to survive any challenges it has so far faced, have also seldom been seriously challenged.

A POSTMODERN SOCIETY?

The result is that, to a degree unparalleled in other advanced capitalist societies, everyday life and especially work life is lived in the same *Kigyôshugi* terms as those present in the official discourse. On the general point, as on so many others, I agree with Harootunian (1989). What we differ over is how to classify the society thus described – is it modern or postmodern? To my mind and notwithstanding the weakness of citizenship rights within it, which is normally taken as indicative of a pre-modern condition, such a society is rather definitely modern rather than postmodern as Harootunian seems to suggest. That is, Japan is modern in the rather particular and to me negative sense that, like the United States in the 1950s, it is a society in which the then 'modernisationists' dream of 'the end of ideology' (understood as the marginalisation of anti-capitalist ideologies [Bell 1988]) has come very close to realisation.

This difference between Harootunian and myself also perhaps arises because we differ over the meaning of that omnipresent but ill-defined and therefore elusive notion 'the postmodern condition' (Woodiwiss 1991). In my somewhat deviant view and as applied to social formations as a whole rather than simply to their aesthetic and philosophical realms, this condition which was first described by Lyotard (1985) is a possibly temporary and definitely conjunctural phase rather than an epochal shift. More specifically, it is a condition in which a hegemonic ideology remains in place but, in mute recognition of capitalism's inability to deliver what had been promised in its name, is no longer acted upon, even by those who consciously promote it – hence the pervasive sense of things not being what they seem that is the street-level indicator of the condition's presence. As I have argued at length elsewhere (Woodiwiss 1991), there are good reasons for thinking that this condition obtains in the United States.

In Japan there exists a pertinent and widely acted upon distinction between *tatemae* and *honne* (in this context, the difference between saying what is expected and saying what one really thinks), which can even allow for the two levels of discourse to be in contradiction with one another. However, Japanese capital remains very definitely in an ascendant position and the promises contained in the anyway very ambivalently modernistic discourses of *Kigyôshugi* therefore retain great plausibility. The result is that, whilst very few Japanese are the workaholic dupes of western mythology, there is very little in the way of that pervasive ideological scepticism and even cynicism which obtains when a hegemonic ideology has become a totem that has lost its magic. The consequence is that there are very few postmodern 'nomads' amongst those who unselfconsciously preface so many of their explanations to those whom, corroboratively, they insist on referring to as *gaijin* (outsiders), with the formula, 'We Japanese'. Indeed, the only voluntary *ronin* (itinerent masterless samurai) these days are those students whose parents can afford to allow them to repeatedly retake the entrance exams to prestigious universities in the hope that examination success will ultimately lead to a job in an equally prestigious company or ministry.

The degree of hegemony that Japan exhibits may appear remarkable but, ironically, it is also somewhat fragile. This is because in many and maybe most workplaces *Kigyôshugi* appears to coexist, apparently symbiotically, with a pervasive, personalistic but surprisingly under-researched factionalism. Personal observation and anecdotal evidence suggest that this factionalism is endemic within Japanese institutions, that it dominates the less formal side of life within them and that it occasionally disrupts their more formal processes, including their relations with outside bodies. One day such divisions just might once again coincide with the division between labour and capital, as they did briefly in the course of the 'production control' strikes of the immediate postwar period. If such a coincidence did ever recur and especially if any such development was accompanied by the electoral defeat of the LDP, labour might thereby obtain access to the very political power that it has lacked even a surrogate for since the 1940s, but which is perhaps prefigured in the form taken by the *shunto*. The availability of some such access is essential if labour is to have any chance of reversing the derogation of its legal rights that I have outlined, and which I would suggest is also heavily implicated in such recent derogations of social rights as those which result from the ever closer connection between income level and educational opportunity, as well as between income level and the possibility of choice as regards residential tenure. As both equality of educational opportunity for their children and the possibility of owning homes of their own disappear for urban salarymen, let alone for blue-collar workers, the question as to what constitutes a 'living wage' has once again begun to gain a definite salience in Japanese politics. This is a salience, moreover, that not only carries the possibility of initiating a new questioning of the privilege accorded capital's rights and powers, but also suggests a new and in many ways more authentically Japanese way of reducing trade friction, namely the increasing of employee purchasing power. Unsurprisingly, this, the single most obvious measure that could have been suggested, did not figure in the recommendations that emerged from the recent Structural Impediments Initiative talks between Japan and the United States. Clearly, for all the current talk of Japan's difference, the 'Dodge Line' lives on and with it the shared recognition of the limits that have to be observed if capitalism is to be preserved.

Finally, no matter how strong it may superficially appear and no matter how often it may be repeated, a single signifying thread, such as that represented by *Kigyōshugi*, is still just a single thread. Because the state of political, economic and class relations would, of course, have a significant bearing on the outcome, the consequences of this thread breaking are impossible to predict – except that in the likely absence of the options available in ideologically less integrated and more pluralistic societies, and as in isolated incidents today, any such breakage is probably still likely to be accompanied by a far from postmodern rage, such as that which Harootunian detects in pre-Restoration Japan and which one is unlikely to see the like of elsewhere in the advanced capitalist world. The question 'why?' is one which both those who would derive lessons from Japan and those who have to listen to them would do well to ponder.

NOTE

1 This point and some of its more general theoretical implications are developed in greater detail in Woodiwiss 1990c.

GLOSSARY

assem	mediation
bakufu	shogunate
burakumin	untouchables
chotei	conciliation
daimyo	feudal lords
emphyteusis	an indefinite grant of land given on condition that an annual rent is paid
genro	elder statesmen/advisors
han	clan
ie	household
IRAA	Imperial Rule Assistance Association
JES	'Japanese Employment System'
jomukai	board of directors
jori	commonsense
JSP	Japan Socialist Party
kaiho	section chief
kaisha	large companies
kami	ancestral spirits
kanban	just in time inventory control system
keiretsu	post war industrial-financial combines
Kigyôshugi	enterprisism/belief in intrinsic virtue of the company
kigyô	enterprise
kobun	states of child
kokata	labourers
kokutai	imperial Japanese policy
koseki	registers
LDP	Liberal Democratic Party
LRAL	Labour Relations Adjustment Law
mura	village
nemawashi	system of pre-meeting lobbying
nenko jotetsu	seniority related pay
Nihonjinron	theories of Japaneseness
NLRA	National Labour Relations Act

163

oyabun	status of parent
oyakata	labour subcontractors
PCLL	Public Corporations Labour Law
Rechsstaat	law state
ri	natural law
SCAP	Supreme Commander Allied Powers
seisan kanri	production control strikes
shinden	new land
shitauke	main contractor/sub contractor groups
shonin	urban dynamics
shukko	transfer of employees to related firms
shunto	spring labour offensive
shushigaku	orthodox Tokugawa Confucianistic philosophy
tan nans	trade union federations
tantomin	people in charge of something
tennosei	emperor system ideology
tenno	emperor
THA	Taft–Hartley Act
usufruct	a lifetime right to use and take the fruits of something belonging to another
wa	harmony
zaibatsu	privately owned 'monopolistic' combines

TABLE OF CASES

Translations of all the statutes referred to in the text may be found in *Labour Laws of Japan* [Ministry of Labour, Tokyo 1980]. Unless indicated otherwise, the translations of the cases listed below are to be found in the Gould Collection of Japanese Labour Law Cases held by the Contemporary Japan Centre, University of Essex.

Asahi Broadcasting Case (1976), Central LRC: 64–73.
Fuji Heavy Industry Case (1977), *Rodo Hanrei*, vol. 287: 709.
Goka Roren Case (1960), Central LRC: 89–97.
Japan Mail Order Case (1975), *Rominshu*, vol. 26, no. 3: 451.
Japan v. Kikuchi et al. (1977), *Keishu*, vol. 31, no. 3: 182.
Japan v. Ogawa et al. (1976), *Keishu*, vol. 30, no. 5: 1178.
Japan v. Osawa (1974), *Keishu*, vol. 28, no. 9: 393.
Japan v. Sakane et al. (The Court Worker Incitement Case) (1969), *Keishu*, vol. 23, no. 5: 685 (see also Itoh and Beer 1978: 103–30).
Kanagawa Labour Relations Commission and Yuken Manufacturing Company Ltd. v. National Union of General Workers, Kanagawa Local et al. (1976) *Minshu*, vol. 30, no. 4: 409.
Kotobuki Kenchiku Kenkyusho (Kotobuki Architectural Research Company) Case, (1977), *Rominshu*, vol. 28, no. 3: 223
Mitsui Mining Co. Ltd. and seven Others v. Japan Miners Labor Union and four Others (1957), *Rodo Kankei Minji Saiban Reishu*, vol. 26, no. 5: 870.
Okada v. Japan (1950), *Hanreishu*, vol. 4, no. 11: 2257 (see also Maki 1964: 273–81).
Pan American World Airways Case, (1973) *Rominshu*, vol. 24, no. 6: 669
Taisei Kanko (Hotel Okura) Case (1972), Tokyo Local LRC: 348–52.
Taisei Kanko (Hotel Okura) Case (1975) *Rodo Hanrei*, vol. 221: 32–41.
Tokachi Girls' Commercial High School Case (1952), *Hanreishu*, vol. 4, no. 2: 258 (see also Maki 1964: 282–4).
Tokyo Electric Express Railway Company Case (1951), *Hanreishu*, vol. 5, no. 5: 214 (see also Maki 1964: 285–8).

Toppan Insatsu Disciplinary Dismissal Incident (1957), *Rodo kankei Minji Saibanreishu,* vol. 8, no. 2: 209.

Toyama et al. v. Japan (Tokyo Central Post Office Case) (1966), *Keishu,* vol. 20, no. 8: 901 (see also Itoh and Beer 1978: 85–103).

Toyo Sanso Joint Stock Company Case (1979), *Rominshu,* vol. 30, no. 5: 1002.

Tsuruzono v. Japan (1973), *Keishu,* vol. 27, no. 4: 547 (Tanaka 1976: 806–11).

Yokohama Rubber Case (1970), *Minshu,* vol. 24, no. 7: 1220

For the following cases it was not possible to locate the source:
Nissan Motor Co. Case.
Shuhoko Bus Case (1968).
Teacher's Union President Case (1980).

REFERENCES

Abegglen, J. and Stalk, G. (1985) *Kaisha: The Japanese Corporation*, Basic Books, New York.

Abel, R. L. (ed.)(1982) *The Politics of Informal Justice*, Academic Press, New York.

Abercrombie, N., Hill, S. and Turner, B. (eds)(1990) *Dominant Ideologies*, Unwin Hyman, London.

Akita, G. (1967) *Foundations of Constitutional Government in Modern Japan, 1868–1900*, Harvard University Press, Cambridge, Mass.

Allen, G. C. (1946) *A Short Economic History of Modern Japan, 1867–1937*, Allen and Unwin, London.

Allen, G. C. (1965) *Japan's Economic Expansion*, Oxford University Press, Oxford.

Allinson, G. D. (1975) *Japanese Urbanism*, University of California Press, Berkeley.

Anderson, P. (1974) *Lineages of the Absolutist State*, New Left Books, London.

Aoki, S. (1987) 'A case study of new-type trades unions', mimeo, Department of Sociology, Meiji Gakuin University.

Ayusawa, I. (1966) *A History of Labour in Modern Japan*, East West Center Press, Honolulu.

Banno, J. (1987) 'The formation and collapse of the Meiji constitutional system', Orientation Seminar, 26, Japan Foundation, Tokyo.

Beasley, W. G. (1972), *The Meiji Restoration*, Stanford University Press, Stanford.

Beckmann, G. (1957) *The Making of the Meiji Constitution*, University of Kansas, Lawrence.

Beer, L. W. (1968) 'The public welfare standard and freedom of expression in Japan', in Henderson (1968a).

Beer, L. W. (1984) *Freedom of Expression in Japan*, Kodansha International, Tokyo.

Beer, L. W. and Tomatsu, H. (1975) 'A guide to the study of Japanese law', *The American Journal of Comparative Law*, 23: 284.

Bell, D. (1988) *The End of Ideology*, Harvard University Press, Cambridge, Mass.

Bennett, J. and Ishino, I. (1963) *Paternalism in the Japanese Economy*, University of Minnesota Press, Minneapolis.

Bix, H. (1986) *Peasant Protest in Japan, 1590–1884*, Yale University Press, New Haven.

Bohlander, G. (1987) 'The rights of non-union employees to strike', *Labour Law Journal*, vol. 38, no. 3: 184.

Broadbridge, S. (1966) *Industrial Dualism in Japan*, Frank Cass, London.

Brown, D. M. (1955) *Nationalism in Japan*, University of California Press, Berkeley.

Burks, A. (1966) *The Government of Japan*, Methuen, London.

Chalmers, N. (1989) *Industrial Relations in Japan: The Peripheral Workforce*, Routledge, London.

Chen, P. (1981) *The Formation of the Early Meiji Legal Order*, Oxford University Press, Oxford.

Clark, R. (1979) *The Japanese Company*, Yale University Press, New Haven.

Cohn, N. (1957) *The Pursuit of the Millennium*, Secker and Warburg, London.

Cole, R. (1971) *Japanese Blue Collar: The Changing Tradition*, University of California Press, Berkeley.

Conroy, H., Davis, S. and Patterson, W. (1984) *Japan in Transition*, Associated University Press, London.

Cook, A. and Hayashi, H. (1980) *Working Women in Japan: Discrimination, Resistance and Reform*, Cornell University Press, Ithaca

Craig, A. (1961) *Choshu and Meiji Restoration*, Cambridge University Press, Cambridge.

Crump, J. (1983) *The Origins of Socialist Thought in Japan*, Croom Helm, London.

Curtis, G. (1988) *The Japanese Way of Politics*, Columbia University Press, New York

Cusumano, M. (1985) *The Japanese Auto Industry: Technology and Management at Nissan and Toyota*, Harvard University Press, Cambridge Mass.

Dale, P. (1988) *The Myth of Japanese Uniqueness*, Routledge, London.

De Becker, J. E. (1909) *Annotated Civil Code of Japan*, reprinted by University Publications of America, 1979, Washington.

De Becker, J. (1916) *Elements of Japanese Law*, reprinted by University Publications of America, 1979, Washington.

Denison, E. and Chung, W. (1976) *How Japan's Economy Grew So Fast*, The Brookings Institution, Washington.

Dohse. K., Jurgens, U. and Walsh, T. (1985) 'From Fordism to Toyotaism', *Politics and Society*, vol. 14, no. 2.

Dore, R. (1959) *Land Reform in Japan*, Oxford University Press, London.

Dore, R. (1973) *British Factory, Japanese Factory*, Allen and Unwin, London.

Dore, R. (1986) *Flexible Rigidities: Industrial Policy and Structural Adjustment in the Japanese Economy 1970–80*, The Athlone Press, London.

Dore, R. (1987) *Taking Japan Seriously*, The Athlone Press, London.

Dower, J. (ed.) (1975) *The Origins of the Modern Japanese State: Selected Writings of E. H. Norman*, Pantheon, New York.

Durkheim, E. (1961) *The Elementary Forms of the Regligious Life*, Collier–Macmillan, New York.

Earl, D. M. (1964) *Emperor and Nation in Japan*, University of Washington.

Edelman, B. (1980) 'The legalisation of the working class', *Economy and Society*, vol. 9, no. 1: 50.

Foucault, M. (1970) *The Order of Things*, Tavistock, London.

Foucault, M. (1974) *The Archaeology of Knowledge*, Tavistock, London.

Foucault, M. (1979) *The History of Sexuality*, vol. 1, Penguin, Harmondsworth.

Friedman, D. (1988) *The Misunderstood Miracle*, Cornell University Press, Ithaca.

Fukui, H. (1970) *Party in Power: The Japanese Liberal Democrats and Policy-Making*, University of California, Berkeley.

Fukui, T. (1973) 'Labor–management relations in Japan (II): acts of dispute', Sophia University Socio-Economic Institute Bulletin, no. 50.

Garon, S. (1985) 'State and religion in imperial Japan 1912–45', *Journal of Japanese Studies*, vol. 12, no. 2: 273.

Garon, S. (1987) *The State and Labour in Modern Japan*, University of California Press, Berkeley.

Gluck, C. (1985) *Japan's Modern Myths: Ideology in the Late Meiji Period*, Princeton University Press, Princeton.

Goldthorpe, J. H. (1964) 'Social stratification in industrial society', *Sociological Review*, Monograph 8.

Goldthorpe, J. H. (1980) *Social Mobility and Class Structure in Modern Britain*, Oxford University Press, Oxford.

Gordon, A. (1985) *The Evolution of Labour Relations in Japan*, Harvard University Press, Cambridge, Mass.

Gottdiener, M. and Comninos, N. (eds) (1989) *Capitalist Development and Crisis Theory*, Macmillan, London.

Gould, W. (1984) *Japan's Reshaping of American Labour Law*, MIT Press, Cambridge, Mass.

Hackett, R. (1968) 'Political modernisation and the Meiji *Genro*', in Ward (1968).

Halberstam, D. (1986) *The Reckoning*, Bantam, New York.

Haley, J. O. (1978) 'The myth of the reluctant litigant', *Journal of Japanese Studies*, vol. 4, no. 2: 359.

Haley, J. O. (1982a) 'Sheathing the sword of justice in Japan: an essay on law without sanctions', *Journal of Japanese Studies*, vol. 8, no. 2: 265.

Haley, J. O. (1982b) 'The politics of informal justice: the Japanese experience', in Abel, R. L. (1982).

Haley, J. O. (1986) 'Japanese administrative law: introduction', *Law in Japan*, 19: 1.

Hall, J. W. (1968a) 'A modern monarch for modern Japan', in Ward (1968).

Hall, J. W. (1968b) *Studies in the Institutional History of Early Modern Japan*, Princeton University Press, Princeton.

Hall, J. W. (1985) 'Reflections on Murakami Yasuke's "Ie society as a civilisation"', *Journal of Japanese Studies*, vol. 11, no. 1: 48.

Hall, R. K. (ed. and translator) (1974) *Cardinal Principles of the National Entity of Japan* (Kokutai no Hongi), Croftan Publishing Corporation, Newton, Mass.

Hall, S. and Jaques, M. (1989) *New Times: The Changing Face of Politics in the 1980s*, Laurence and Wishart, London.

Halliday, J. (1976) *A Political History of Japanese Capitalism*, Pantheon, New York.

Hanami, T. (1979) *Labour Law and Industrial Relations in Japan*, Kluwer, Deventer.

Hanami, T. and Blanpain, R. (eds)(1989) *Industrial Conflict Resolution in Market Societies*, Kluwer, Deventer.

Hane, M. (1982) *Peasants, Rebels and Outcasts: The Underside of Modern Japan*, Pantheon, New York

Harari, E. (1973) *The Politics of Labour Legislation*, University of California Press, Berkeley.

Harootunian, H. (1970) *Toward Restoration*, University of California Press, Berkeley.

Harootunian, H. (1974) 'A sense of an ending and the problem of Taisho', in Silberman and Harootunian (1974).

Harootunian, H. (1982) 'Ideology as conflict', in Najita and Korshmann (1982).

Harootunian, H. (1989) 'Visible discourses/invisible ideologies', in Miyoshi and Harootunian (1989).

Henderson, D. F. (ed.) (1968a) *The Constitution of Japan: Its First Twenty Years*, University of Washington Press, Seattle.

Henderson, D. F. (1968b) 'Law and political modernisation in Japan', in Ward (1968).

Henderson, D. F. (1974) '"Contracts" in Tokugawa Japan', *The Journal of Japanese Studies*, vol. 1, no. 1: 51.

Henderson, D. F. (1977) *Conciliation and Japanese Law*, 2 vols, University of Washington Press, Seattle.

Henderson, D. F. (1980) 'Japanese law in English: reflections on translation', *Journal of Japanese Studies*, vol. 6, no. 1: 117.

Henderson, D. F. and Haley, J. (eds)(1978) *Law and Legal Process in Japan*, University of Washington, mimeo.

Hepple, B. (ed.) (1986) *The Making of Labour Law in Europe*, Mansell, London.

Hindess, B. and Hirst, P. (1975) *Pre-Capitalist Modes of Production*, Routledge and Kegan Paul, London.

Hingwan, K. (1990) 'Racism and migrant labour in Japan', M.A. dissertation, Contemporary Japan Centre, The University of Essex.

Hirosuki, K. (1986) 'The reality of enterprise unionism', in McCormack and Sugimoto (1986).

Hirschmeier, J. and Yui, T. (1981) *The Development of Japanese Business*, Allen and Unwin, London.

Hobsbawm, E. (ed.) (1984) *The Invention of Tradition*, Cambridge University Press, Cambridge.

Hoston, G. A. (1987) *Marxism and the Crisis of Development in Prewar Japan*, Princeton University Press, Princeton.

Hozumi, N. (1938) *Ancestor Worship and Japanese Law*, Hokuseido Press, Tokyo.

Ike, N. (1978) *A Theory of Japanese Democracy*, Westview Press, Boulder.

Inagami, T. (1988) *Japanese Workplace Industrial Relations*, The Japan Institute of Labour, Tokyo.

Irokawa, D. (1985) *The Culture of the Meiji Period*, Princeton University Press, Princeton.

Ishida, T. (1988) 'The development of interest groups and the political modernisation of Japan', in Ward (1968).

Ishida, H., Goldthorpe, J. and Erikson, R. (1988) *Intergenerational Class Mobility in Postwar Japan*, Nissan Institute, Oxford.

Ishii, R. (ed.)(1968) *Japanese Legislation in the Meiji Era*, Kasai, Tokyo.

Ishii, R. (1980) *A History of Political Institutions in Japan*, University of Tokyo Press, Tokyo.

Ishimine, K. (1974) *A Comparative Study of Judicial Review under American and Japanese Constitutional Law*, University Microfilms, Ann Arbor.

Ito, H. (1889) *Commentaries of the Constitution of the Empire of Japan*, Igirisu-Horitsu Gakko, Tokyo.

Itoh, H. (1970) 'How judges think in Japan', *The American Journal of Comparative Law*, vol. 18: 775.

Itoh, H. and Beer, L. (eds) (1978) *The Constitutional Case Law of Japan: Selected Supreme Court Decisions 1961–70*, University of Washington Press, Seattle.

Japan Institute of Labour (1983) *Highlights in Japanese Industrial Relations*, vol. 1, Tokyo.

Japan Institute of Labour (1988) *Highlights in Japanese Industrial Relations*, vol. 2, Tokyo.

Jessop, B. (1982) *The Capitalist State*, Martin Robertson, Oxford.

Jessop, B. (1987) 'Conservative regimes and the transition to post-Fordism in western Europe' in Gottdiener, M. and Comninos, N. (1989).

Johnson, C. (1975) 'Japan: who governs? An essay on official bureaucracy', *Journal of Japanese Studies*, vol. 2, no. 1: 1.

Johnson, C. (1982) *MITI and the Japanese Miracle*, Stanford University Press, Stanford.

Johnson, C. (1986) 'Structural corruption and the advent of machine politics in Japan', *Journal of Japanese Studies*, vol. 12, no.1: 1.

Kahn-Freund, O. (1977) *Labour and the Law*, Stevens, London.

Kamata, S. (1983) *Japan in the Passing Lane*, Allen and Unwin, London.

Kawanishi, H. (1986) 'The reality of enterprise unionism', in McCormack, G. and Sugimoto, Y. (eds)(1986).

Koike, K. (1988) *Understanding Industrial Relations in Modern Japan*, Macmillan, Basingstoke.

Kokutai no Hongi (1974) 'Cardinal principles of the national entity of

Japan', in R.K. Hall (ed.) Croftan Publishing Corporation, Newton, Mass.

Komiya, F. (1986) 'A comparative analysis of the law of dismissal in Great Britain, Japan and the USA.', ST/ICERD Discussion Paper, London School of Economics.

Kondo, D. (1990) *Crafting Selves: Power, Gender, and Discourse in a Japanese Workplace*, University of Chicago Press, Chicago.

Koshiro, K. (1985) 'The reality of dualistic labor market in Japan: scarcity of good employment opportunities and industrial relations', *East Asia*, vol. 2: 33.

Kuwahara, Y. (1988) 'Industrial relations and human resource management in Japan', in Kuwahara, Y. *et al.* (eds) (1988).

Kuwahara, Y. (1989) *The Industrial Relations System in Japan: A New Interpretation*, The Japan Institute of Labour, Tokyo.

Kuwahara, Y., Bamber, G. and Lansbury, R. (1988) *Industrial Relations in Advanced Countries: Factors of Maturity and Change*, mimeo, Japan Institute of Labour, Tokyo.

Large, S. (1972a) *The Rise of Labour in Japan*, Sophia University Press, Tokyo.

Large, S. (1972b) *The Yuaikai: 1912–19*, Sophia University Press, Tokyo.

Large, S. (1981), *Organised Workers and Socialist Politics in Interwar Japan*, Cambridge University Press, Cambridge.

Large, S. (1983) 'Buddhism and political renovation in prewar Japan', *Journal of Japanese Studies*, vol. 9, no. 1: 33.

Leader, S. (1988) 'Two models of collective bargaining in a single European market', mimeo, The Department of Law, University of Essex.

Lee, C. and De Vos, G. (eds) (1981) *Koreans in Japan*, University of California Press, Berkeley.

Lehmann, J. P. (1982) *The Roots of Modern Japan*, Macmillan, London.

Levine, S. (1958) *Industrial Relations in Postwar Japan*, University of Illinois Press, Urbana.

Levine, S. (1982) 'Japanese industrial relations: an external view', in Sugimoto, Y. *et al.* (1982).

Lincoln, E. (1988) *Japan: Facing Economic Maturity*, The Brookings Institution, Washington.

Littler, C. (1982) *The Development of the Labour Process in Capitalist Societies*, Heinemann, London.

Livingston, J., Moore, J. and Oldfather, F. (eds) (1973) *The Japan Reader: Imperial Japan*, Pantheon, New York.

Lublinskaya, A. D. (1968) *French Absolutism: The Crucial Phase, 1620–1629*, Cambridge University Press, Cambridge.

Lyotard, J. F. (1985) *The Postmodern Condition*, Manchester University Press, Manchester.

McCormack, G. and Sugimoto, Y. (eds)(1986) *Democracy in Contemporary Japan*, Hale and Iremonger, Sydney.

McLaren, W. W. (1914) 'Japanese Government Documents', Transactions of the Asiatic Society of Japan, XLII: 1.

McLaren, W. W. (1965) *A Political History of Japan During the Meiji Era*, Frank Cass, London.

Macmillan, C. J. (1985) *The Japanese Industrial System*, de Gruyter, Berlin.

Maki, J. (1962) *Government and Politics in Japan: The Road to Democracy*, Thames and Hudson, London.

Maki, J. (ed.) (1964) *Court and Constitution in Japan*, University of Washington Press, Seattle.

Maki, J. (Trans., ed.) (1980) *Japan's Commission on the Constitution: The Final Report*, University of Washington Press, Seattle.

Marshall, B. (1967) *Capitalism and Nationalism in Prewar Japan*, Stanford University Press, Stanford.

Marshall, T. H. (1962) *Sociology at the Crossroads*, Heinemann, London.

Marsland, S. E. (1989) *The Birth of the Japanese Labour Movement*, University of Hawaii Press, Honolulu.

Maruo, M. (1986) 'The development of the welfare mix in Japan', in R. Rose and R. Shiratori (eds) *The Welfare State: East and West*, Oxford University Press: New York.

Maruyama, M. (1969) *Thought and Behaviour in Modern Japanese Politics*, Oxford University Press, London.

Matsushita, K. (1984) *Not for Bread Alone: A Business Ethos, A Management Ethic*, PHP Institute Inc., Kyoto.

Mehren, A. T. van (ed.) (1963) *Law in Japan*, Harvard University Press, Cambridge, Mass.

Miller, F. O. (1965) *Minobe Tatsukichi: Interpreter of Constitutionalism in Japan*, University of California Press, Berkeley.

Minear, R. (1970) *Japanese Tradition and Western Law*, Harvard University Press, Cambridge, Mass.

Minear, R. (1980) 'Orientalism and the far east', *Journal of Asian Studies*, vol. 39, no. 3: 507.

Mitchell, R. H. (1976) *Thought Control in Prewar Japan*, Cornell University Press, Ithaca.

Miyoshi, M. and Harootunian, H. (eds) (1989) *Postmodernism and Japan*, Duke University Press, Durham, N. C.

Moore, B. Jnr. (1966) *Social Origins of Dictatorship and Democracy*, Penguin, Harmondsworth.

Moore, J. (1983) *Japanese Workers and the Struggle for Power*, University of Wisconsin Press, Madison.

Morishima, M. (1982) *Why has Japan 'Succeeded'?*, Cambridge University Press, Cambridge.

Mukai, K and Toshitani, N. (1967) 'The progress and problems of compiling the Civil Code in the early Meiji era', *Law in Japan*, 1.

Murakami, Y. (1984) '*Ie* society as a pattern of civilisation', *Journal of Japanese Studies*, vol. 10, no. 1: 279.

Murakami, Y. (1985) '...Response to criticism', *Journal of Japanese Studies*, vol. 11, no. 2: 401.

Murakami, Y. (1987) 'The Japanese model of political economy', in Yamamura, K. and Yasuba, Y. (1987).

Najita, T. (1974) *The Intellectual Origins of Modern Japanese Politics*, University of Chicago Press, Chicago.

Najita, T. and Korshmann, J. V. (eds)(1982) *Conflict in Modern Japanese History: The Neglected Tradition*, Princeton University Press, Princeton.

Nakamura, H. (1960) *The Ways of Thinking of Eastern Peoples*, Unesco, Tokyo.

Nakamura, K. (1962) *The Formation of Modern Japan: As Viewed from Legal History*, The Centre for East Asian Cultural Studies, Tokyo.

Nakamura, T. (1983) *Economic Growth in Prewar Japan*, Yale University Press, New Haven.

Nakane, C. (1970) *Japanese Society*, Penguin, Harmondsworth.

Nakano, T. (1923) *The Ordinance Power of the Japanese Emperor*, The Johns Hopkins Press, Baltimore.

Nakayama, I. (1975) *Industrialisation and Labour Management Relations in Japan*, Japan Institute of Labour, Tokyo.

Napier, R. (1982) 'The transformation of the Japanese labour market, 1894–1937', in Najita and Korshmann (1982).

Nevins, T. (1984) Labour Pains and the Gaijin Boss: Hiring, Firing and Managing the Japanese, *Japan Times*, Tokyo.

Nitta, M. (1988) 'Structural changes and enterprise-based unionism in Japan', in Kuwahara, Y. *et al.* (eds)(1988).

Noda, Y. (1976) *Introduction to Japanese Law*, University of Tokyo Press, Tokyo.

Norman, E. H. (1940) *Japan's Emergence as a Modern State*, Institute of Pacific Relations, New York.

Ohta, T. (1988) 'Works rules in Japan', *International Labour Review*, vol. 127, no. 5: 627.

Okada, T. (1983) 'The state and society in history as seen from the history of the Japanese labour union movement', *Annals of the Institute of Social Science*, vol. 26.

Oppler, A. C. (1976) *Legal Reform in Occupied Japan: A Participant Looks Back*, Princeton University Press, Princeton, New Jersey.

Osawa, M. (1988) 'Structural transformation and industrial relations in the Japanese labour market', in Kuwahara, Y. *et al.* (eds)(1988).

Pascale, R. and Athos A. (1983) *The Art of Japanese Management*, Penguin, Harmondsworth.

Passin, H. (1965) *Society and Education in Japan*, Teachers' College and East Asian Institute, Columbia University.

Patrick, H. (ed.)(1976) *Japanese Industrialisation and Its Social Consequences*, University of California Press, Berkeley.

Patrick, H. and Rohlen, T. (1987) 'Small-scale family enterprises', in Yamamura, K and Yasuba, Y. (1987).

Patrick, H. and Rosovsky, H. (eds) (1976) *Asia's New Giant: How the Japanese Economy Works*, The Brookings Institution, Washington.

Piore, M. and Sabel, C. (1984) *The Second Industrial Divide*, Basic Books, New York.

Pittau, J. (1967) *Political Thought in Early Japan, 1868–1889*, Harvard University Press, Cambridge, Mass.

Quigley, H. and Turner, J. (1956) *The New Japan*, University of Minnesota Press, Minneapolis.

Rohlen, T. (1974) *For Harmony and Strength: Japanese White Collar Organisation*, University of California Press, Berkeley.

Said, E. (1979) *Orientalism*, Vintage, New York.

Sawada, J. T. (1968) *Subsequent Conduct and Supervening Events*, University of Tokyo Press, Tokyo.

Scalapino, R. A. (1953) *Democracy and the Party Movement in Prewar Japan*, University of California, Berkeley.

Scalapino, R. A. (1968) 'Elections and political modernisation in prewar Japan', in Ward (1968).

Scalapino, R. A. (1983) *The Early Japanese Labour Movement*, Institute of East Asian Studies, Berkeley.

Sheldon, C. D. (1958) *The Rise of the Merchant Class in Tokugawa Japan*, Russel and Russel, New York.

Shimada, H. (1980) *The Japanese Employment System*, Japan Institute of Labour, Tokyo.

Shimada, H. (1988) 'New challenges to contemporary industrial relations in Japan', in Kuwahara, Y. *et al.* (eds)(1988).

Shimodaira, H. (1985) 'Notes on some general features of the Japanese union movement', mimeo, Faculty of Economics, Shinshu University.

Siemes, J. (1968) *Herman Roesler and the Making of the Meiji State*, Sophia University Press, Tokyo.

Silberman, B. (1982) 'The bureaucratic state in Japan: the problem of authority and legitimacy', in Najita and Korshmann (1982).

Silberman, B. and Harootunian, H. (eds) (1974) *Japan in Crisis: Essays on Taisho Democracy*, Princeton University Press

Smith, T. C. (1959) *The Agrarian Origins of Modern Japan*, Stanford University Press, Stanford.

Steiner, K., Krauss, E. and Flanagan, S. (1980) *Political Opposition and Local Politics in Japan*, Princeton University Press, Princeton.

Steven, R. (1983) *Classes in Contemporary Japan*, Cambridge University Press, Cambridge.

Stevens, C. R. and Takahashi, K. (eds)(1975) *Materials on Japanese Law*, mimeo, Columbia University Law School.

Stevens, C. R. (1971) 'Modern Japanese law as an instrument of comparison', *The American Journal of Comparative Law*, vol. 19: 665–84.

Stockwin, J. A. (1982) *Japan: Divided Politics in a Growth Economy*, Weidenfeld & Nicolson, London.

Storry, R. (1960) *A History of Modern Japan*, Penguin, Harmonsworth.

Sugeno, Y. (1979) 'Public employee strike problem and its legal regulation in Japan', *Current Studies in Japanese Law*, Center for Japanese Studies, University of Michigan, Ann Arbor.

Sugeno, K. (1988a) 'Japanese industrial relations system and a paradigm of labour–management law,' in Kuwahara, Y. *et al.* (eds)(1988).

Sugeno, K. (1988b) 'The doctrine of union democracy as applied to enterprise unions: another pluralism in Japanese labor law', *Japan Labor Bulletin*, vol. 27, no. 7.

Sugeno, K. (1989) '*Shukko*: an aspect of the changing labor market in Japan', *Japan Labor Bulletin*, vol. 28, no. 4.

Sugeno, K. (no date) 'Resolution of shop floor disputes in Japan', mimeo, Faculty of Law, University of Tokyo.

Sugimoto, Y., Shimada, H. and Levine, S. (1982) *Industrial Relations in Japan*, Japanese Studies Centre, Melbourne.

Sugimoto, Y. and Mouer, R. (1984) *Images of Japanese Society*, Routledge, London.

Suwa, Y. (1989) 'Unfair labor practices involving JR firms', *Japan Labour Bulletin*, vol.28, no. 11.

Tabata, H. (1989) 'Changes in plant level trade union organisations: a case study of the automobile industry', *Annals of the Institute of Social Science*, vol. 31.

Taira, K. (1970) *Economic Development and the Labour Market in Japan*, Columbia University Press, New York.

Takanashi, (1989) *Shunto*, Japan Labour Institute, Tokyo.

Takayanagi, K. (1963) 'A century of innovation: developments in Japanese law', in Tanaka (1976).

Takayanagi, K. (1976) 'A century of innovation: the development of Japanese law, 1868–1961', in Tanaka (1976).

Tanaka, H. (ed.)(1976) *The Japanese Legal System*, University of Tokyo Press, Tokyo.

The Joint Trade Union Committee Supporting Mr Tanaka's Trial, 'Statement and Materials', mimeo, Tokyo.

Therborn, G. (1984) 'New questions of subjectivity', *New Left Review*, 143: 97.

Toshitani, N. (1976) 'Japan's Modern Legal System: Its Formation and structure'. *Annals of the Institute of Social Science*, vol. 17.

Totsuka, H. (1984) 'Rationalisation and the Japanese trade unions', *Bulletin of the Socialist Research Centre*, no. 7.

Totten, G. O. (1974) 'Japanese industrial relations at the crossroads: the great Noda strike of 1927–28', in Silberman and Harootunian (1974).

Townsend, P. (1979) *Poverty in the United Kingdom*, Penguin, Harmondsworth.

Toyoda, T. (1969) *A History of Pre-Meiji Commerce in Japan*, Japan Cultural Society, Tokyo.

Tsunoda, R. (ed.) *Sources of the Japanese Tradition*, Columbia University Press, New York.

Turner, B. (1986) *Citizenship and Capitalism: the Debate Over Reformism*, Unwin Hyman, London.

Ukai, N. and Nathanson, N. (1968) 'Protection of property rights and due process of law in the Japanese Constitution', in Henderson (1968a).

Umegaki, M. (1988) *After The Restoration: The Beginnings of Japan's Modern State*, New York University Press, New York.

Upham, F. (1987) *Law and Social Change In Postwar Japan*, Harvard University Press, Cambridge, Mass.

Uyehara, G. (1910) *The Political Development of Japan: 1867–1909*, Constable, London

Vogel, E. (1963) *Japan's New Middle Class*, University of California Press, Berkeley.

Wada, K. (1977) 'The administrative court under the Meiji Constitution', *Law in Japan*, 10.

Ward, R. E. (1957) 'The origins of the present Japanese Constitution', in Tanaka, H. (1976).

Ward, R. E. (ed.)(1968) *Political Development in Modern Japan*, Princeton University Press, Princeton.

White, H. (1973) *Metahistory*, Johns Hopkins University Press, Baltimore.

White, J. (1970) *The Soka Gakkai and Mass Society*, Stanford University Press, Stanford.

Wilkinson, T. O. (1965) *The Urbanisation of Japanese Labour, 1868–1955*, University of Massachusetts Press, Amherst.

Wolferen, K. van (1989) *The Enigma of Japanese Power: People and Politics in a Stateless Nation*, Macmillan, London.

Wolpe, H. (ed.)(1980) *The Articulation of Modes of Production*, Routledge, London.

Woodiwiss, A. (1985a) 'Law, discourse and transpositioning', *International Journal of the Sociology of Law*, vol. 13: 61.

Woodiwiss, A. (1987a) 'The discourses of production (pt.1): law, industrial relations and the theory of ideology', *Economy and Society*, vol. 16, no. 3: 275.

Woodiwiss, A. (1987b) 'The discourses of production (pt.2): the contract of employment and the emergence of democratic capitalist law in Britain and the United States', *Economy and Society*, vol. 16, no. 4: 441.

Woodiwiss, A. (1989) 'Paradox lost (and with it Japan's uniqueness)', *Pacific Review*, vol. 2, no. 1: 38.

Woodiwiss, A. (1990a) *Rights* v. *Conspiracy: A Sociological Essay on the History of Labour Law in the United States*, Berg, Oxford.

Woodiwiss, A. (1990b) *Social Theory After Post-Modernism: Rethinking Production, Law and Class*, Pluto, London.

Woodiwiss, A. (1990c) 'Rereading Japan: capitalism, possession and the necessity of hegemony', in Abercrombie, Hill and Turner (1990).

Woodiwiss, A. (1991) '*Postmodanizumu*: Japanese for (and against) postmodernism', *Theory, Culture and Society*, vol. 8, no. 4.

Woodiwiss, A. (1991) *An American Fall: The Forgetting of Modernism in the Postwar United States*, Pluto, London.

Woronoff, J. (1983) *Japan's Wasted Workers*, Lotus Press, Tokyo.

Woronoff, J. (1986) *Politics: the Japanese Way*, Macmillan, London.

Wright, E. O. (1985) *Classes*, Verso, London.

Yamamura, K. (1967) *Economic Policy in Postwar Japan*, University of California Press, Berkeley.

Yamamura, K. (1982) 'Success that soured: administrative guidance and cartels in Japan', in Yamamura, K. (1982).

Yamamura, K. (ed.) (1982) *Policy and Trade Issues of the Japanese Economy*, University of Washington Press, Seattle.

Yamamura, K. and Yasuba, Y. (1987) *The Political Economy of Japan: The Domestic Transformation*, Stanford University Press, Stanford.

INDEX